ACE Group Fitness Specialty Book

Youth
Fitness

By Avery D. Faigenbaum, Ed.D., and Wayne L. Westcott, Ph.D.

AMERICAN COUNCIL ON EXERCISE®
www.acefitness.org

Library of Congress Control Number: 2001093669

First edition
ISBN 1-890720-11-9
Copyright © 2001 American Council on Exercise (ACE)
Printed in the United States of America.

ABCDEF

Distributed by:
American Council on Exercise
P.O. Box 910449
San Diego, CA 92191-0449
(858) 535-8227
(858) 535-1778 (FAX)
www.acefitness.org

Managing Editor: Daniel Green
Design & Production: Karen McGuire
Manager of Publications: Christine J. Ekeroth
Assistant Editor: Jennifer Schiffer
Index: Bonny McLaughlin
Models: Rita LaRosa Loud & Christine Lee

Acknowledgments:
Thanks to the entire American Council on Exercise staff for their support and guidance through the process of creating this manual.

NOTICE
The fitness industry is ever-changing. As new research and clinical experience broaden our knowledge, changes in programming and standards are required. The authors and the publisher of this work have checked with sources believed to be reliable in their efforts to provide information that is complete and generally in accord with the standards accepted at the time of publication. However, in view of the possibility of human error or changes in industry standards, neither the authors nor the publisher nor any other party who has been involved in the preparation or publication of this work warrants that the information contained herein is in every respect accurate or complete, and they are not responsible for any errors or omissions or the results obtained from the use of such information. Readers are encouraged to confirm the information contained herein with other sources.

P01-033

REVIEWERS

Diane E. (De) Raynes is the project manager for research and professional development at the National Association for Sport and Physical Education (NASPE), in Reston, Virginia. She received her Masters and Specialist degrees from Virginia Polytechnic Institute and State University in Virginia. Prior to joining NASPE, Raynes taught high school physical education for 30 years in Fairfax County, Virginia, and coached track and field, cross country, basketball, and field hockey.

Stephen J. Virgilio, Ph.D., is an associate professor in the department of physical education at Adelphi University, Garden City, New York. He is the author of two textbooks and has published over 50 articles in professional journals. Dr. Virgilio is co-author of *Active Start*, NASPE's physical activity guidelines for pre-school children.

TABLE OF CONTENTS

INTRODUCTION

The American Council on Exercise (ACE) is pleased to include Youth Fitness as a Group Fitness Specialty Book. As the industry continues to expand, evolve, and redefine itself, the youth population has emerged as one in need of well-designed classes and expert leadership. It has become apparent that guidelines and criteria should be established so that this population can be taught to exercise both safely and effectively. The intent of this book is to educate and give guidance to fitness professionals that wish to teach youth classes. As with all areas of fitness, education is a continual process. ACE recognizes this is a broad subject requiring serious study and we encourage you to use the References and Suggested Readings as well as the recommended Web sites to further your knowledge.

Chapter One

Introduction to Youth Fitness

Years ago, there was less concern about physical activity programs for youth because long walks to school, physical chores in the afternoon, and regular participation in school-based physical education classes kept young bodies healthy and strong. But today, computers and video games have decreased youngsters' need to move, and there are fewer safe places for them to play. Even more unfortunate is that some schools view physical education as an expendable part of the educational curriculum, and there is a growing attitude that recess should be cut back or eliminated. Clearly, physical inactivity among youth has become a major public health concern. At present, our nation spends billions of dollars each year on lifestyle-related diseases, and the likelihood of a significant increase is both real and alarming.

The bottom line is that a sedentary lifestyle during childhood and adolescence increases the risk of developing major health problems, such as heart disease, diabetes, and osteoporosis, later in life. Opportunities must be created for boys and girls of all ages and abilities to be physically active. Rather than focus entirely on fitness skills and sports performance, you can gear youth programs toward lifelong physical activity and having fun. For instance, while well-organized, quality sports programs have their place, team sports such as football and field hockey are difficult to carry over into adulthood and are not necessarily the best solution for decreasing the hypoactivity of American youth. However, you can activate kids' lives by encouraging them to expend calories throughout the whole day while running, jumping, lifting, kicking, and balancing. The key is for you to value the importance of incorporating physical activity into children's lives, and to help them develop healthy habits that persist into adulthood.

In this book, the term *children* refers to boys and girls that have not yet developed secondary sex characteristics (roughly up to the age of 11 in girls and 13 in boys). This period of development is also referred to as *preadolescence*. The term *teenager* (or adolescent) refers to a period of time between childhood and adulthood and includes girls ages 12 to 18 years and boys ages 14 to 18 years. For ease of discussion, the terms *youth, youngsters,* and *kids* are broadly defined in this text to include both children and teenagers.

Current Fitness Status

Millions of youth in the United States are currently at risk for developing degenerative diseases in their adult years because they are not active enough. The percentage of overweight boys and girls has more than doubled during the past two decades (National Center for Health

Statistics, 2000), and of youngsters ages five to 15 who are overweight, 61% have one or more cardiovascular disease risk factors, and 27% have two or more (Freedman et al., 1999). Results of the 1999 California Physical Fitness test indicate that a staggering 80% of fifth-, seventh-, and ninth-graders tested were unable to meet minimum standards to be considered physically fit (National Association for Sport and Physical Education, 2000). In the United States, television viewing, "surfing" the Internet, and playing video games contribute substantially to the amount of time youth spend in sedentary pursuits. On average, young people between the ages of two and 18 spend an astounding four hours a day using electronic media (e.g., watching television, playing video games, or using a computer) (Kaiser Family Foundation, 1999). By high school graduation, it is likely that a youngster will have spent more time in front of the television than in school (Strasburger, 1992).

The negative health consequences associated with childhood obesity and physical inactivity include hypertension and the appearance of atherosclerosis and type 2 "adult onset" diabetes among children and teenagers. Furthermore, since both positive and negative behaviors established at a young age have a high probability of persisting into adulthood, it is likely that inactive kids will become inactive adults (Janz et al., 2000; Trudeau et al., 1999). As such, preventive health efforts that increase physical activity during childhood and adolescence will likely have favorable health benefits in later years. In the long run, health promotion strategies that ensure healthy levels of physical activity among children and teenagers could help to maintain the progress that has been made over the past few decades in reducing deaths from cardiovascular disease. The

Healthy People 2010 report includes participation in physical activity as one of the nation's 10 leading health indicators (U.S. Department of Health and Human Services, 2000).

Participation in all types of vigorous physical activity declines with age, and the decline is greater in females than males (Figure 1). Participation in moderate-intensity physical activity, such as walking and bicycling, also declines with age. Data from national transportation surveys indicate that walking and bicycling by children and teenagers ages five to 15 dropped 40% between 1977 and 1995 (National Personal Transportation Survey, 1997). Unfortunately, this trend typically continues through adulthood and the senior years.

Figure 1
Age-related decline in vigorous physical activity

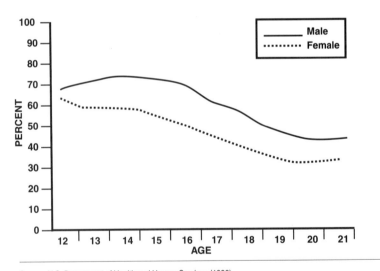

Source: U.S. Department of Health and Human Services (1996).

The Surgeon General's Report, titled *Physical Activity and Health* (U.S. Department of Health and Human Services, 1996), highlighted disturbing trends in physical activity among young people in the United States:

- Only about one-half of young people regularly participate in vigorous physical activity. One-fourth report no vigorous physical activity.
- Only about one-fourth of young people walk or bicycle (i.e., light-to-moderate activity) nearly every day.
- Participation in all types of physical activity declines strikingly as age increases.
- Daily enrollment in physical education among high school participants has decreased.
- Physical inactivity is more common among females than males.

Benefits of Youth Fitness

Now more than ever you have the information to justify physical activity programs for children and teenagers because of the numerous physical and psychosocial benefits documented through research (U.S. Department of Health and Human Services, 1996). Regular participation in a physical activity program helps to build and maintain healthy bones, muscles, and joints, enhance motor performance skills, reduce fat and control weight, and lower blood cholesterol, prevent or delay the development of high blood pressure, and reduce the risk of developing diabetes. Regular participation in physical activity also promotes feelings of well-being, reduces symptoms of anxiety and depression, and simply makes boys and girls feel better about themselves.

Well-organized youth activity programs characterized by caring and competent instruction also give children and teenagers the opportunity to make new friends and experience the enjoyment of physical activity. Kids who engage regularly in physical activity tend to do better in school, and a growing body of evidence suggests that health-related behaviors acquired during childhood and adolescence are more likely to be carried into adulthood. Therefore, a youngster who enjoys physical activity and learns how to live a physically active life is more likely to become an active adult.

Youth Fitness Guidelines

The steepest decline in physical activity for boys and girls occurs during their teenage years. Why? The number one reason is that exercise is not fun anymore. Other factors include poor instruction and too much pressure to perform from parents and coaches. What you need to realize is that young people have different needs than adults and are active in different ways. Watching boys and girls on a playground supports the premise that the natural physical activity pattern of boys and girls is characterized by sporadic bursts of energy with brief periods of rest as needed.

Children and teenagers should be encouraged to be physically active daily, or nearly every day, as part of play, games, school, and work. However, the intensity or duration of the activity is less important than burning calories and establishing a habit of physical activity at an early age. This does not mean that exercising within a target heart rate range (i.e., 60% to 80% of age-predicted maximal heart rate) is not beneficial, but rather that you should not expect kids to exercise in the same manner as adults. The bottom line is that physical activity does not have to be vigorous to be beneficial, nor do children and teenagers need to participate in structured training programs.

While many organizations have developed physical activity guidelines, the Children's Lifetime Physical Activity Model

(C-LPAM) is best suited for younger populations and is more consistent with current public health objectives (Figure 2) (Corbin et al., 1994). A second widely accepted set of physical activity guidelines developed just for teenagers (Sallis et al., 1994), is similar to C-LPAM. Unlike previous recommendations for adults that focus on fitness and performance, the C-LPAM is an age-specific model that addresses the amount of physical activity necessary to produce health benefits associated with reduced morbidity and mortality. Sports-related components of physical fitness such as agility, balance, and speed are important, but the health-related components of physical fitness, including aerobic endurance, muscular strength, and flexibility, should be the focus of your youth activity programs.

Figure 2

Children's Lifetime Physical Activity Model (C-LPAM)

The Health Standard: A Minimum Activity Standard

Frequency:	Daily. Frequent activity sessions (three or more) each day.
Intensity:	Moderate. Alternating bouts of activity with rest periods as needed, or moderate activity such as walking or riding a bike to school.
Time:	Duration of activity necessary to expend at least 3 to 4 kcal/kg/day. Equal to caloric expenditure in 30 minutes or more of active play or moderate sustained activity that may be distributed over three or more activity sessions.

The Optimal Functioning Standard: A Goal for All Children

Frequency:	Daily. Frequent activity sessions (three or more) each day.
Intensity:	Moderate-to-vigorous. Alternating bouts of activity with rest periods as needed, or moderate activity such as walking or riding a bike to school.
Time:	Duration of activity necessary to expend at least 6 to 8 kcal/kg/day. Equal to caloric expenditure in 60 minutes or more of active play or moderate sustained activity that may be distributed over three or more activity sessions.

Source: Corbin, C. et al. (1994).

While the minimal recommendations for expending calories are similar between C-LPAM and the traditional adult model (3 to 4 kcal/kg/day), the C-LPAM recommends that youth alternate moderate-to-vigorous physical activity with brief periods of rest and recovery as needed, since young people will rarely perform continuous vigorous exercise. In fact, continuous moderate-to-vigorous physical activity lasting more than five minutes without rest or recovery is rare among children because they have short attention spans and are concrete rather than abstract thinkers.

The C-LPAM also suggests that, optimally, children expend 6 to 8 kcal/kg/day, since physical activity patterns tend to decline as we age and most youngsters have more time to exercise than adults. For instance, a girl who weighs 40 kg (88 lbs.) should expend at least 120 kcal per day (40 kg x 3 kcal/day) and optimally 320 kcal per day (40 kg x 8 kcal/day). Many scientific and governmental organizations, including the National Association for Sport and Physical Education and the 2000 Dietary Guidelines for Americans, also recommend that young people accumulate at least 60 minutes per day of moderate-to-vigorous physical activity (U.S. Department of Agriculture and U.S. Department of Health and Human Services, 2000). This recommendation is based in part on the observation that 60 minutes or more of daily physical activity may be needed to offset the growing trend in childhood obesity. Further, since children and teenagers need physical activity for normal growth and development, and need a substantial amount of time to develop basic motor patterns, they may require more physical activity than adults. While additional benefits are associated with even greater amounts of physical activity, the benefit decreases somewhat beyond 6 to 8 kcal/kg/day.

The C-LPAM provides a nonthreatening and undemanding standard that even sedentary children can achieve with a modest commitment to physical activity. Games and activities, walks to school, chores around the house, and physical movements on a playground are examples of lifestyle activities that are consistent with the C-LPAM. Simply reducing sedentary leisure pursuits such as television viewing and video games can increase physical activity and help youngsters lose weight.

Remember that the focus of the C-LPAM is on the accumulation of physical activity throughout the day rather than continuous bouts of physical activity performed at a predetermined intensity. While continuous moderate-to-vigorous physical activity is not physiologically harmful, it is not the most appropriate method of training for children. Children do not see the benefit of prolonged periods of high-intensity training, and cardiovascular adaptations such as increasing aerobic capacity are less noticeable in children compared to older populations. As such, children are less likely to see improvements and are more likely to lose interest. However, as boys and girls enter their teenage years, some may want to follow the traditional target heart-rate model to enhance fitness or sports performance. It is your responsibility to assess the needs and abilities of all participants, and to carefully review what changes they expect as a result of your youth fitness program.

Parent and Community Involvement

The troubling consequences of physical inactivity among youth are evident. To help children and teenagers develop lifelong healthy habits and lead active lifestyles, parents need to model and support participation in enjoyable activity programs, and communities need to provide instruction, programs, and services that promote physical activity. We live in a society that makes it easy to be sedentary, so parents and community organizations need to coordinate their efforts, maximize resources, and get involved in the promotion of lifelong participation in physical activity among young people. Clearly, families and communities can have a powerful influence on a youngster's health and activity habits.

Parents should become educated about the importance of youth physical activity, and communities should provide young people with a range of developmentally appropriate activities that make it easy and safe to be active. Special attention must also be given to the development of programs for those in greatest need, including girls and racial/ethnic minorities. Since physical activity has become a voluntary effort, it is our shared responsibility to develop and promote youth physical activity programs that are safe, enjoyable, guided by qualified instructors, and supported by cultural norms that make partic-ipation desirable. You can work with parents and community organizations to help promote physical activity and active lifestyles in children and teenagers.

Chapter Two

Fitness Fundamentals

Youth fitness programs are a good way for boys and girls to learn new skills, be with friends, and feel good about themselves. Although most youth programs traditionally focus on sports performance, you should encourage—but not force—youth to participate in a variety of activities that develop locomotive (e.g., running), non-locomotive (e.g., twisting), and manipulative (e.g., catching) skills. Instead of focusing entirely on competitive sport activities, youth fitness programs should also include non-competitive, age-specific games and activities that keep everyone moving most of the time.

While competently supervised and responsibly coached youth sport programs provide an opportunity for youngsters to be physically active, not all boys and girls enjoy intense competition, and many aspiring young athletes are ill-prepared for the demands of sport practice and games. Kids with inadequate motor skills and poor musculoskeletal health are likely to drop out of sports because of frustration, embarrassment, failure, and possibly injury. Furthermore, emphasizing sport skills as opposed to fundamental fitness abilities not only discriminates against youth whose motor skills are not as well developed, but it may also lead to sports-related overuse injuries such as tendonitis, shin splints, and stress fractures (Micheli et al., 2000). Regular conditioning helps to strengthen supporting structures and prevent fatigue during practice and games, which helps to prevent injury. Some health professionals estimate that 50% of overuse injuries in youth sports could be prevented if more emphasis was placed on preparatory fitness conditioning as opposed to sports-specific training (Smith et al., 1993).

Perhaps if our playgrounds were busier, the need to develop fundamental fitness abilities would not be so crucial. But unfortunately, other than sleeping, television viewing accounts for the greatest amount of leisure time during childhood. Your job is to develop interventions that substantially increase the amount of time youth spend being physically active. Since most physical activity among youth occurs outside of the school setting, you are in a unique position to serve as a positive role model and enhance the health and well-being of children and teenagers.

Health and Safety

Due to age, size, and maturational differences, the individual needs and concerns of all the youngsters in your exercise program must be addressed. Although it is not mandatory for apparently healthy children and teenagers to have a medical examination, parents should complete a health and activity questionnaire for each child prior to participation. The questionnaire should ask about pre-existing medical ailments (e.g., asthma, diabetes), previous injuries, recent surgery, allergies, and the activity interests of each participant. If necessary, a

physician should screen any youngster with known or suspected
health problems, including illness or injury, prior to participation.

Prior to every class, consider conducting a quick "health check"
by asking participants how they feel. Pay particular attention to
any signs of illness or unusual aches or pains. Also, remind
youngsters about program rules (e.g., listen and follow directions,
try your best, be a good sport) and safety tips (e.g., proper
footwear, shoes tied, no gum chewing during class). Occasionally,
youngsters, like adults, may come to class feeling tired or lazy. On
those days, allow them to "take it easy" or perform a modified
workout that may include exercising at a lower intensity for a
shorter period of time.

All youth activity programs should take place in an exercise
environment that is clean and free of clutter (Figure 3). In many
cases, activity-related injuries can be prevented if safety is made a

priority. Take time before every class to be sure equipment is stored appropriately, the room is well-lit, and the floor is clean. Due to the exploratory nature of some children, you may need to remove or disassemble any broken pieces of equipment from the exercise area. Overcrowded and poorly designed fitness centers increase the likelihood that a youngster may get hurt, or bump into a piece of equipment or another participant.

A Safety Action Plan should be developed and periodically reviewed in the case of a serious emergency. The plan should include the location of first-aid equipment and telephones, standardized first-aid procedures, entry routes for emergency personnel, responsibilities of each staff person, and documentation materials. Recognizing the need for safer youth sports and activities, the American Red Cross and the United States Olympic Committee joined forces to develop a Sports Safety Training Course for coaches and youth fitness leaders. This course includes information on injury prevention, CPR, and first aid, and is delivered through local chapters of the American Red Cross.

Summary of Safety Tips

- Screen all participants for illnesses or injuries that may limit or prevent safe participation.
- Regularly inspect all activity areas and ensure that equipment is stored in a safe place.
- Explain safety rules to participants and parents.
- Ensure youngsters wear appropriate footwear and attire for all physical activities.
- Work with participants to develop a sense of responsibility.
- Develop and periodically practice a Safety Action Plan.
- Maintain current CPR and first-aid certification.

Program Considerations

A erobic, strength, and flexibility exercises should be part of a well-rounded fitness program for children and teenagers. However, certain strength-building exercises such as the barbell squat, bench press, and overhead press require spotters and appropriate starting weights. Youth fitness leaders should be nearby in case of a failed repetition and the use of an unloaded barbell, light dumbbells, or even a long wooden dowel will allow each child to develop proper exercise technique before the weight is increased. While children and teenagers should be encouraged to stretch, the exercises shown in Figures 4–8 should be avoided due to the excessive stress placed on the developing musculoskeletal system.

Figure 4
Contraindicated exercise: Back-bend

Figure 5
Contraindicated
exercise: Windmill

Figure 6
Contraindicated
exercise: W-position

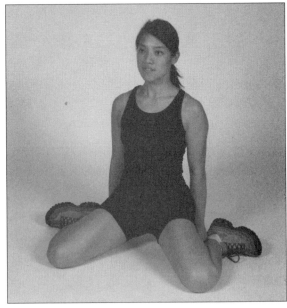

Figure 7
Contraindicated exercise: Yoga plow

Figure 8
Contraindicated exercise: Hurdler's stretch

Equipment and supplies for your youth fitness programs will vary depending upon the objectives of your program, available space, and your budget. Several equipment companies manufacture weight-training equipment specifically designed for children and lightweight dumbbells and medicine balls are readily available. Game supplies such as playground balls, foam balls, jump ropes, beanbags, balloons, hula hoops, and parachutes are relatively inexpensive and available from fitness stores and physical education equipment companies. Keep in mind, however, that simply purchasing child-friendly equipment and supplies will not necessarily result in a successful youth fitness program. Experienced youth fitness leaders who genuinely care about kids will make your program shine.

Leadership and Instruction

The challenges associated with getting kids off the couch should be met with enthusiastic leadership and qualified instruction. When leading a youth activity class, encourage participants to ask questions, listen to their concerns, and allow them to provide suggestions for games and activities. Some youngsters dislike and fear activities that they perceive as forced upon them by an adult. Attempting to sell physical activity to boys and girls on the basis that it can enhance their quality of life is a losing proposition. Rather, increasing a youngster's flexibility or muscle strength should be the byproduct of creative programming and enthusiastic leadership.

It is important for you to understand the uniqueness of childhood and adolescence, and to genuinely appreciate the fact that youth are active in different ways. When working with children, you need to relate to them in a positive manner and understand how they think. In short, do not forget about the value of play, which is one of the ways in which we all learn. In some cases, instructors who are terrific with adults may lack the patience and understanding to work with children and teenagers. Staff training sessions and youth fitness seminars can help you learn to work effectively with children and teenagers. The youth fitness tips below may help you develop safe, worthwhile, and enjoyable programs for boys and girls of all ages and abilities.

Tips for Youth Fitness Leaders

1. Treat youngsters respectfully and listen to their concerns.
2. Provide opportunities for boys and girls of all ages and abilities to regularly engage in physical activity.
3. Play down competition and focus on intrinsic values such as skill improvement, personal successes, and excitement.
4. Recognize individual differences and capabilities of all youth.
5. Learn the names of all youngsters in your program.
6. Give kids an opportunity to perform a new skill while you observe and provide feedback. Most children and teenagers learn best by doing.
7. Provide competent and caring supervision at all times.
8. Offer a variety of creative activities and avoid regimentation.
9. Be a good role model and lead a healthy lifestyle.
10. Encourage parents to support youth physical activity programs.

Fitness Education

Adult exercise guidelines and training philosophies (e.g., no pain, no gain) should not be imposed on children and teenagers. Youth programs should focus on fundamental fitness activities and having fun. While some adults may enjoy 30 minutes of continuous exercise on a stepping machine, most children and teenagers (especially those who are sedentary and overweight) do not enjoy this kind of activity. Physically active youth often raise their heart rates into their target zones but, unlike adults, they often choose to exercise in an interval-type pattern characterized by haphazard increases and decreases in physical activity.

Instead of competitive games in which youth are chosen for teams, expand their fitness opportunities by developing age-appropriate games and activities in which every child is a winner. A major objective of youth fitness programs is for physical activity to become a habitual part of kids' lives that hopefully persists into adulthood. You must therefore strive to increase youngsters' self-confidence in their physical abilities.

The focus of youth fitness programs should be on positive experiences. Even though society often preaches the importance of winning, the major reason youngsters engage in physical activity is to have fun. Provide clear instructions so that children and teenagers can experience success and develop a sense of mastery of selected motor skills. Program goals should not be limited to increasing muscle strength, but should include teaching youngsters about their body, developing a personalized workout program, and sparking an interest in lifelong physical activity.

Nutrition Education

American youth today are fatter than ever before. In addition to promoting physical activity, fitness professionals should recognize the importance of encouraging youngsters to give their bodies the right fuel. Children and teenagers need proper nutrition to maintain their health and optimize their performance. But in many more families than ever before nutritious home-cooked meals are being replaced with fast foods that are high in fat, salt, and sugar. Poor nutrition, which is defined as meals and snacks that are too high in fat and too low in essential nutrients, is a major health concern affecting many children and teenagers.

Youngsters need to eat a well-balanced diet that is high in fruits, vegetables, and whole grains to ensure ample energy and to provide them with essential vitamins, minerals, antioxidants, and fiber. Fats should be restricted to about 20% to 25% of total calories, and carbohydrates and proteins should make up about 55% and 20%, respectively, of the total caloric intake. As illustrated in the food guide pyramid (Figure 9), a strong diet has a base of whole grains, fruits, and vegetables.

Figure 9

The Food Guide Pyramid

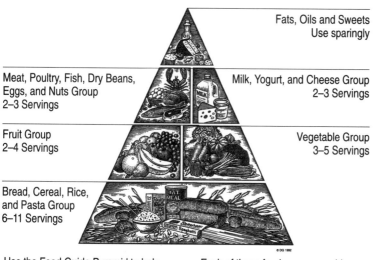

Fats, Oils and Sweets
Use sparingly

Meat, Poultry, Fish, Dry Beans, Eggs, and Nuts Group
2–3 Servings

Milk, Yogurt, and Cheese Group
2–3 Servings

Fruit Group
2–4 Servings

Vegetable Group
3–5 Servings

Bread, Cereal, Rice, and Pasta Group
6–11 Servings

Use the Food Guide Pyramid to help you eat better every day ... the Dietary Guidelines way. Start with plenty of Breads, Cereals, Rice, and Pasta; Vegetables; and Fruits. Add two to three servings from the Milk group and two to three servings from the Meat group.

Each of these food groups provides some, but not all, of the nutrients you need. No one food group is more important than another — for good health you need them all. Go easy on fats, oils and sweets, the foods in the tip of the Pyramid.

Source: U.S. Department of Agriculture.

Although five servings of fruits and vegetables may seem like a lot, meeting this recommendation is quite easy. One medium piece of fruit, 1/4 cup of dried fruit, 1/2 cup of cooked vegetables, or 3/4 cup of 100% fruit or vegetable juice are all equal to one serving. Often, this can be accomplished by adding fruit to morning cereal, lettuce and tomato to a sandwich at lunch, and a salad and baked potato to an evening meal. The items at the top of the pyramid (fats, oils, and sweets) should be used sparingly. Do not ask youngsters to eliminate foods they truly enjoy; instead, encourage them to balance foods high in fat with selections from the fruit, vegetable, and grain groups.

Healthy food choices provide children and teenagers with the necessary energy, nutrients, and building blocks to maintain an active lifestyle. Further, teaching boys and girls to eat right during childhood and adolescence may increase the likelihood that they continue to make similar choices as adults. You can counter the current high-fat snack attack with alternatives that give children and teenagers an opportunity for better health. Educate by example, provide healthy snacks, and recognize that regular physical activity and proper nutrition are needed for a happy and healthy future.

Also keep in mind that children and teenagers need to drink several glasses of water (or healthy alternatives such as fruit juice or low-fat milk) every day. Encourage all participants to drink water before, during, and after every class. Since children respond to dehydration with an excessive increase in body core temperature, make every effort to ensure that they arrive fully hydrated and drink frequently during class. Providing individual water bottles to participants reminds them to drink regularly even when they are not thirsty. Also, take drink breaks about every 15 to 20 minutes during prolonged activities. Since children and teenagers often underestimate their fluid needs during exercise, it is particularly important to enforce water breaks during youth activity programs.

Chapter Three

Basics of
Youth Fitness Training

S afe and productive youth fitness programs improve muscular strength, cardiovascular endurance, and joint flexibility. When designing such programs, focus on proper training procedures and appropriate exercise selection.

Strength Exercise:
Misconceptions and Facts

F strength training legitimate concerns or unfounded fears? This section examines several prevalent misconceptions about preadolescent strength training, and presents well-researched guidelines for developing safe, effective, and efficient resistance-exercise programs for boys and girls.

Misconception: Children may experience bone growth plate damage as a result of strength training.
Fact: Based on medical reports, there has never been an incidence of bone growth plate damage during strength-training studies conducted with children. In fact, just the opposite is true. Progressive resistance exercise is the best way to enhance musculoskeletal development in pre-adolescents. A recent study showed significant increases in bone mineral density for nine-year-old girls who completed a one-year program of regular strength training and aerobic exercise (Morris et al., 1997).

Misconception: Children cannot increase muscle strength because they do not have enough testosterone.
Fact: Although testosterone certainly enhances strength development, it is not essential for achieving strength gains. After all, women and elderly individuals experience impressive improvements in muscle strength even though they have very little testosterone. As shown in Table 1, 10-year-old boys and girls who participated in a twice-a-week strength-training program made overall strength gains of almost 75% after just two months of exercise (Faigenbaum et al., 1993). Although the non-training control group increased their strength by 13% through normal growth and development, the exercise group experienced almost six times as much strength improvement.

Table 1 Changes in muscle strength for exercise and control subjects after eight weeks of strength exercise (23 subjects, mean age 10 years).

	EXERCISE GROUP (N = 14)			CONTROL GROUP (N = 9)		
	10 RM Strength (kg)			10 RM Strength (kg)		
	Pre	Post	% Change	Pre	Post	% Change
Leg Extension	12.9	21.2	64.5*	12.1	13.8	14.1
Leg Curl	10.4	18.5	77.6*	12.0	13.6	13.2
Chess Press	15.2	25.0	64.1*	13.4	15.0	12.5
Overhead Press	7.5	14.1	87.0*	7.8	8.8	13.1
Biceps Curl	4.7	8.3	78.1*	4.8	5.3	12.2
Mean % Change			74.3			13.0

Significant change (p<0.01).
10 RM = the weight with which an individual can perform 10 repetitions.

Reprinted, by permission, from Faigenbaum, A.D., Zaichkowsky, L.D., Wescott, W.L., Micheli, L.J., & Fehlandt, A.F. (1993). The effects of a twice-a-week strength training program on children. *Pediatric Exercise Science*, 5 ,4, 339 – 346.

Misconception: Children cannot increase muscle mass because they do not have enough testosterone.

Fact: Because gains in muscle strength have a neurological component, it has been assumed that all strength-training improvements achieved by children are attributable to motor learning rather than muscle development. However, a strength-training study with fifth-grade school children showed otherwise (Westcott et al., 1995). As presented in Table 2, the 11-year-old boys and girls who performed strength exercise twice a week for eight weeks added 2½ pounds of lean (muscle) weight. This result was significantly greater than the 1½-pound increase in lean (muscle) weight experienced by a matched control group who did not strength train. Even though children, women, and elderly exercisers have little testosterone, they can still achieve modest increases in muscle tissue through properly performed strength training, and muscle development may occur in preadolescents beyond that associated with normal growth and maturation.

Table 2   Changes in body composition for exercisers and control subjects during an eight-week assessment period (42 subjects, mean age 11 years).

Group	% Fat Change	Lean Weight Change (lbs.)	Fat Weight Change (lbs.)
Exercise	-2.7*	+2.5*	-3.0*
Control	-1.9*	+1.5	-1.4*

*Significant change (p<0.01).

Reprinted, by permission, from Wescott, W.L., Tolken, J., & Wessner, B. (1995). School-based conditioning programs for physically unfit children. *Strength and Conditioning*, 17, 2, 5 – 9.

Misconception: Children's strength gains are temporary and produce no permanent strength advantage over untrained peers. *Fact:* It is true that children, like adults, lose strength after discontinuing their strength-training program. However, the rate of strength loss is much lower than you might expect, especially in the upper-body muscles. In a study examining the effects of detraining, 10-year-old boys and girls completed two months of strength training followed by two months of no strength training (Faigenbaum et al., 1996). A control group performed no strength exercise during the four-month assessment period. As shown in Figure 10, the exercise group attained a 41% increase in chest-press strength during the two-month training program. And while they lost almost half of their strength gain during the two-month detraining period, they were still significantly stronger than the control subjects who gained some strength through normal growth and development processes.

Figure 10

Changes in chest press and leg extension strength for exercise and control subjects during eight-week training and eight-week detraining periods (24 subjects,
mean age 10 years).

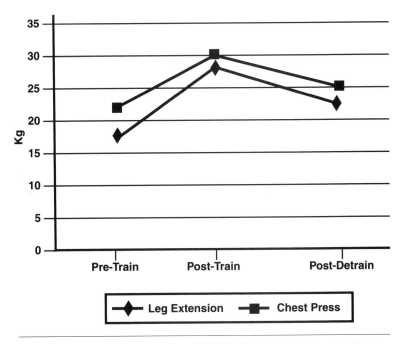

Adapted, by permission, from Faigenbaum, A.D. et al. (1996, 2). The effects of strength training and detraining on children. *Journal of Strength and Conditioning*, 10, 2, 109 – 114.

Misconception: Children should perform body-weight
exercises like pull-ups and push-ups rather than weight-
training exercises such as lat pull-downs or bench presses.
Fact: Critics have argued that strength training is an unnatural
physical activity and that children do not like to exercise with
external resistance. They feel strongly that children should use
their own body weight in calisthenic-type exercises. Indeed,
training with body-weight exercises such as pull-ups and push-
ups can be productive if body weight provides an appropriate
resistance for a child's muscular ability.

Unfortunately for most adults and children, their body weight is simply too heavy to permit safe and productive strength exercise. For example, data from the President's Council on Physical Fitness and Sports reveals that only one of every two youngster's can perform even a single pull-up, making this body-weight exercise unsuitable for training purposes.

Properly performed push-ups present a similar problem for most preadolescents. Even if children can complete 10 push-ups in good form, they are unable to progressively increase the exercise resistance. Certainly they can perform more push-ups with further training, but adding exercise repetitions is not nearly as effective for building muscle strength as gradually increasing the training resistance.

With respect to safety, it is far less risky for children to perform 10 pull-downs with half their body weight (e.g., 35-pound weightstack) than to struggle unsuccessfully with a single pull-up (e.g., 70-pound body weight). The major advantages of weight training over body weight exercise are: 1) the resistance can be adjusted to match children's current muscular ability, and 2) the resistance can be progressively increased as children's strength improves.

Youth Strength Training

The following basic strength-training guidelines are recommended for children between seven and 15 years of age. They are applicable to all types of resistance equipment, including weightstack machines, hydraulic machines, pneumatic machines, barbells, dumbbells, resistance bands, rubber tubing, and even medicine balls. Although specific to youth, these recommendations are relatively consistent with the American College of Sports Medicine 2000 guidelines for adult and senior strength training.

Training Resistance

The basic rule for selecting an appropriate training resistance is to fatigue the target muscles within about 60 seconds (typically 10 to 15 good repetitions). Most children can complete between 10 and 15 controlled repetitions with 70% of their maximum resistance, which represents a simple and safe means for determining a desirable training load.

Training Repetitions

Research has demonstrated that preadolescents achieve greater muscle strength and endurance when they perform about 13 to 15 repetitions with moderate weightloads (Faigenbaum et al., 1999). As presented in Table 3, participants who performed 13 to 15 repetitions per set made greater strength gains in both the leg extension and bench press exercises than participants who performed six to eight repetitions per set with relatively heavy weightloads.

Table 3 Effects of an eight-week youth strength-training program using higher repetitions and lower weightloads vs. using lower repetitions and higher weightloads (43 subjects, mean age 8 years).

Variable	Control Group (No training)	Low rep/high weightload group (6–8 reps)	High rep/low weightload group (13–15 reps)
Leg Extension Strength	+13.6%	+31.0%	+40.9%
Chest Press Strength	+4.2%	+5.3%	+16.3%
Leg Extension Endurance	+3.7 reps	+8.7 reps	+13.1 reps
Chest Press Endurance	+1.7 reps	+3.1 reps	+5.2 reps

Reprinted, by permission, from Faigenbaum, A.D. et al. (1999). The effects of different resistance training protocols on muscular strength and endurance development in children, *Pediatrics*, 104, 5.

Training Speed

Once you determine the correct resistance, it is essential that the repetitions be performed properly. Use controlled exercise speed, with approximately two seconds for each lifting movement and approximately two to three seconds for each lowering movement. This emphasizes muscle effort rather than momentum, ensures safe training experiences, and enhances exercise effectiveness. Uncontrolled movements indicate the training resistance is too heavy.

Training Range

Encourage young trainees to perform full-range movements on every repetition of each exercise. Do not permit partial actions, but insist on full-range effort through the positions of joint flexion and joint extension. Short movement ranges indicate that the training resistance is too heavy.

Training Progression

The most important factor for improving muscle strength is to progressively increase the training resistance. This is the essence of the overload principle, but resistance must be added in a gradual and systematic manner. Use the same weightload until the child can complete 15 good repetitions, and then increase the resistance by 5% to 10%. For example, if a teenager completes 15 good dumbbell squats with 50 pounds, he should add 2½ to 5 pounds for his next workout. Of course, this may be difficult to do with fixed-weight dumbbells, necessitating an increase from two 25-pounders to two 30-pounders.

Training Sets

Excellent results have been attained in youth strength-training programs using one, two, and three sets of each training exercise. As a rule, children and young exercisers should perform about 12 total sets per training session. This can be accomplished by performing one set each of 12 different exercises, two sets each of six separate exercises, or three sets each of four different exercises. When performing multiple sets, children should rest one to two minutes between successive sets of exercise.

Training Exercises and Frequency

Children should train all their major muscle groups, including the quadriceps, hamstrings, gluteals, pectoralis major, latissimus dorsi, deltoids, upper trapezius, abdominals, spinal erectors, biceps, and triceps. While single muscle exercises can be easily performed on well-designed, youth-sized weightstack machines, dumbbells and medicine balls are highly effective for working many muscle groups with a few basic exercises. A youngster's activities should include a minimum of one and a maximum of three weekly strength workouts. The seven exercises presented in Table 4 and Figures 11–17 address most of the major muscle groups.

Table 4 Seven exercises that address most major muscle groups.

Exercise	Major Muscle Involvement
Dumbbell Squat Tip: Do not let knees move forward past toes.	Quadriceps, hamstrings, gluteals
Dumbbell Bench Press Tip: Do not drop dumbbells to down position.	Pectoralis major, triceps
Dumbbell Bent-over Row Tip: Do not arch back.	Latissimus dorsi, biceps
Dumbbell Overhead Press Tip: Keep torso erect with lower back flat.	Deltoids, triceps, upper trapezius
Dumbbell Curl Tip: Do not use torso movement to complete exercise.	Biceps
Trunk Curl Tip: Only lift head and shoulder blades off mat.	Rectus abdominis
Trunk Extensions Tip: Do not hyperextend at top position.	Spinal erectors

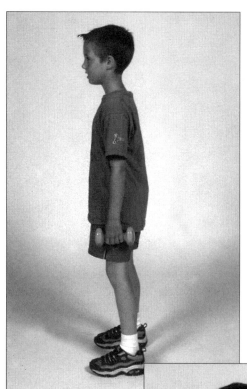

Figure 11
Dumbbell
squat

a. Start position

b. Ending position

Figure 12
Dumbbell
bench
press

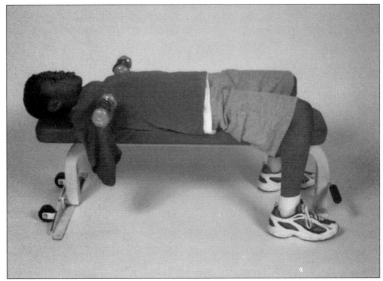

a. Start position

b. Ending position

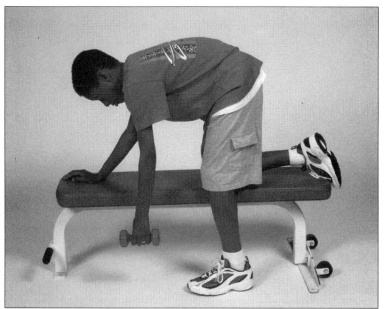

Figure 13
Dumbbell
bent-over
row

a. Start position

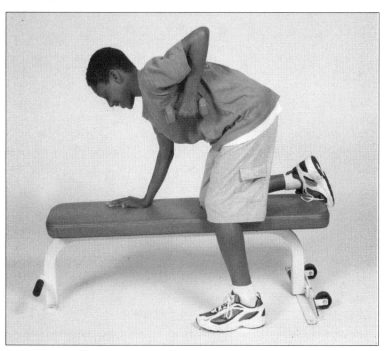

b. Ending position

Figure 14
Dumbbell
overhead
press

a. Start position

b. Ending position

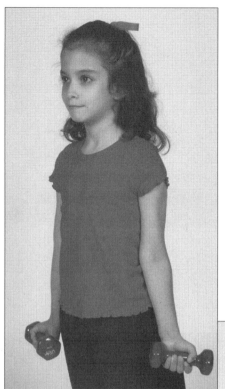

Figure 15
Dumbbell
curl

a. Start position

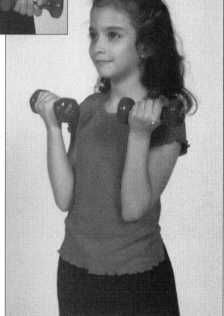

b. Ending position

Figure 16
Trunk curl

a. Start position

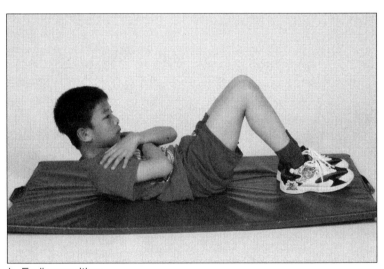

b. Ending position

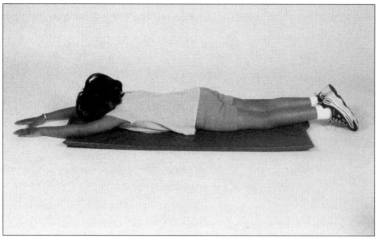

Figure 17
Trunk extension; alternate sides

a. Start position

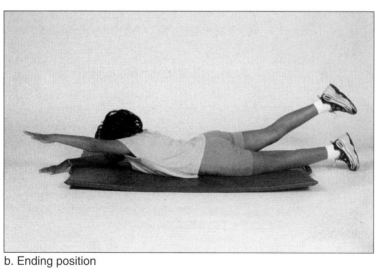

b. Ending position

Youth Endurance Training

Adults are advised to perform regular endurance exercise to increase their aerobic capacity and decrease their risk of cardiovascular disease. Endurance training provides many physiological benefits: the heart becomes a stronger pump, the circulatory system becomes a more efficient blood distributor, and the blood becomes a better oxygen transporter. However, while these impressive internal adaptations are important to many adults, they are not a motivation to exercise for most boys and girls.

Unfortunately, children typically view endurance exercise as an unpleasant activity to avoid whenever possible. Their general pattern of energy expenditure is stop-and-go games in which they run fast and rest, run fast and rest. Although they can comply with the adult model for cardiovascular conditioning if compelled to do so, it makes good sense to modify endurance exercise activities to better match young people's physical and mental characteristics.

The following basic endurance-training guidelines are recommended for children between seven and 15 years of age. They are applicable to all types of aerobic activities, including running, cycling, stepping, rowing, and swimming.

Training Frequency

The American College of Sports Medicine (2000) calls for at least three days per week of endurance training. This is a reasonable recommendation that can easily be achieved by most boys and girls, as long as they perceive the exercise activities to be interesting and enjoyable. Given the opportunity, children will be active in their own way, as evidenced by their enthusiastic participation in recess and physical education classes during their elementary school years.

Training Duration

According to the American College of Sports Medicine (2000), an acceptable endurance exercise session for adults requires between 20 and 60 minutes of continuous or intermittent aerobic activity (minimum of 10-minute bouts). Generally speaking, higher-effort exercises such as running are performed for shorter durations (e.g., 20 to 40 minutes per session), and lower-effort exercises such as walking are continued for longer durations (e.g., 40 to 60 minutes per session). Because most children will not complete a 20-

minute session of continuous endurance training, you will need to make modifications to ensure exercise compliance.

Experience indicates that young people can remain physically active for more than 30 minutes as long as the training session is punctuated with brief rest periods. In other words, they will perform relatively high-level exercise for sufficient duration, given periodic breaks to recover and recharge. Research reveals only small reductions in children's heart rate during the brief non-exercise periods (Faigenbaum, 2001). Therefore, stop-and-go games or activities that alternate higher-effort and lower-effort segments are recommended, as they increase children's likelihood of completing the exercise session.

Training Intensity

As indicated in the previous section, aerobic conditioning may be attained by performing higher-intensity exercise for shorter durations (e.g., 20 to 40 minutes) or lower-intensity exercise for longer durations (e.g., 40 to 60 minutes). The standard means of assessing exercise intensity in adults is heart-rate monitoring, and the American College of Sports Medicine (2000) guidelines call for 60% to 90% of maximum heart rate throughout the training session.

In one respect, heart-rate monitoring is problematic for young people who have great difficulty finding and counting their pulse during exercise. On the other hand, there is little need for children to check their heart-rate response, as they typically remain well within their training zone throughout the entire activity session. Research shows average heart rates around 150 to 170 beats per minute during the aerobic-activity period, and heart rates above 130 beats per minute during the strength-training period (Faigenbaum, 2001).

Another method for measuring teenagers' exercise intensity is the Borg Scale of Perceived Exertion (1982), which rates effort level numerically from very light exertion to very heavy exertion. Generally, however, simple observation is sufficient for determining children's physical output during their training sessions. As long as they participate in the standard exercise program and maintain reasonable flow with the class activities, they typically meet the criteria for cardio-vascular conditioning.

Class Format

Classes should include a 20- to 30-minute strength-training session between two 15- to 20-minute endurance exercise periods. The aerobic segments include locomotion skills with music (e.g., walking, running, skipping, jumping, hopping, stepping), some calisthenics (e.g., jumping jacks, trunk curls, push ups), a few flexibility exercises (e.g., stretches with ropes and lightweight bars), and many apparatus activities (e.g., medicine balls, resistance bands, hoops, cones, steps, playground balls, beach balls). Play all kinds of physically active but non-competitive games to keep the children moving and motivated without fear of failure.

The key to successful participation seems to be instructor involvement. Lead the class activities and perform essentially all of the aerobic exercises along with the children. This role-model approach is highly effective for eliciting enthusiastic and energetic responses from the boys and girls.

Youth Flexibility Training

Although children are typically more flexible than adults, many young people have less than desirable levels of joint mobility. Enhanced flexibility may help children perform better in games, sports, and recreational activities. For this reason, include both static and dynamic stretching exercises in your youth fitness classes.

Have children perform a couple of standard static stretches, such as the seated hamstrings stretch and standing calf stretch, in which they hold the stretched position for several seconds (Figures 18–24). However, emphasize dynamic flexibility through exercises incorporating ropes, lightweight bars, hoops, and playground balls, as the participants find this more interesting and enjoyable. For example, two participants standing back-to-back may hand off a playground ball between their legs and over their heads, alternately stretching their lower back and abdominal muscles, as well as their shoulder joint muscles. Another alternative is to hand off the ball from side-to-side, thereby stretching midsection and shoulder joint muscles.

Joint flexibility is also emphasized in many locomotor activities, such as skipping and hopping. For example, ask the group to lift their knees high when they skip and hop, providing some dynamic stretching for the hip extensor muscles.

Summary of Youth Flexibility-training Guidelines

Children are likely to experience flexibility benefits:
• through a few standard static-stretching exercises.
• through dynamic stretching components of various locomotor skills and activities utilizing ropes, lightweight bars, hoops, and play-ground balls.
• when they are prompted to exaggerate specific movement patterns, such as lifting the knees high when skipping or hopping.

Additional Fitness Program Components

It is always advisable to incorporate warm-up and cool-down activities into each exercise session. Perform about 15 minutes of group games that include running, jumping, and large muscle movements before and after the standard exercise program. Stretching exercises should be included during the final few minutes of the warm-up and cool-down periods.

Figure 18
Sitting
hamstring
stretch

Figure 19
Standing
calf stretch

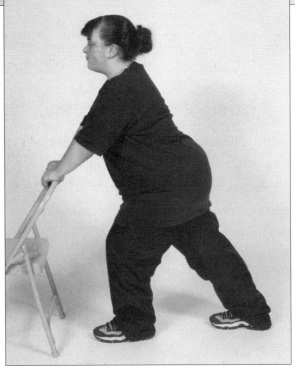

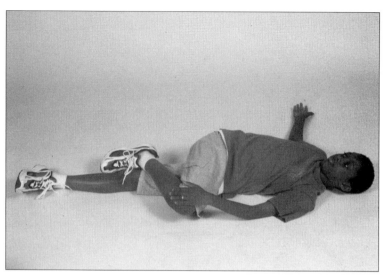

Figure 20
Low-back
and hip
stretch

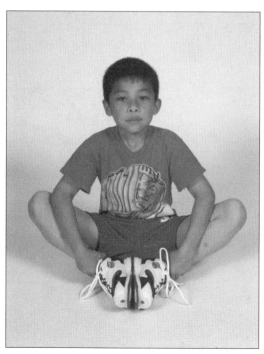

Figure 21
Inner thigh
stretch

Figure 22
Chest
stretch

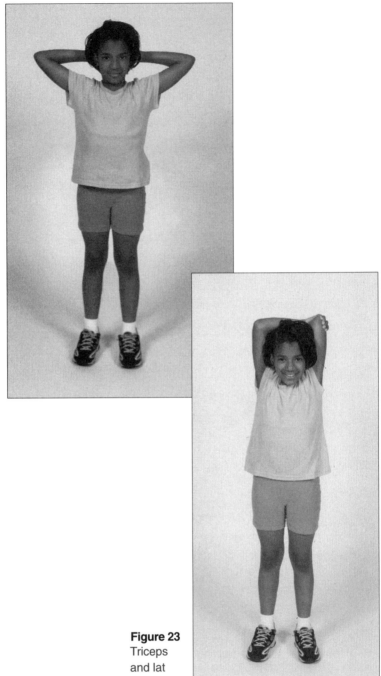

Figure 23
Triceps
and lat
stretch

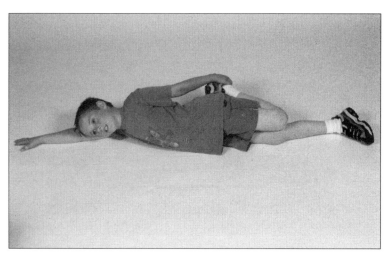

Figure 24
Quadriceps stretch

Chapter Four

Teaching Children Effectively

Most adults who are motivated to exercise require little more than occasional instruction and supervision to maintain a regular training program. Children, on the other hand, are typically more interested in free-play activities than in organized exercise sessions, and they need both education and motivation to exercise correctly and consistently.

Your main objective should be to give every participant a positive and productive exercise experience each training session. The following 10 instructional guidelines are highly effective in this regard. Consider incorporating as many of these teaching techniques as practical into each youth fitness class.

1. Clear Training Objectives

Your first priority in every class is to let the children know exactly what you expect them to accomplish during the exercise session. They should clearly understand each training objective so they can direct their efforts toward achieving it. The best approach is to simply state the day's training objective at the beginning of each class.

Example: "Today's training objective is to perform 10 perfect dumbbell curls for your biceps muscles."

2. Concise Instruction With Precise Demonstration

Do you remember the "show and tell" sessions from elementary school? They were such a simple and successful means for children to communicate information with other children. The same principals work equally well for adults to communicate information with children. Tell youth exactly how to do the exercise as concisely as possible. Then, show them precisely how to perform the exercise with perfect technique. Do not neglect the demonstration, no matter how easy the exercise seems to you. Research indicates that modeling may be the most effective means for influencing participant behavior (Westcott, 1980). This is particularly important in the area of strength exercise, which may be unfamiliar to most boys and girls.

Example: "Perform the dumbbell curl with a straight body position and your elbows glued to your sides. Move only your forearms as you curl the dumbbells from your thighs to your chest. Watch me demonstrate proper form in the dumbbell curl exercise."

3. Attentive Supervision

Many children lack confidence in their physical ability and are understandably reluctant to perform exercises on their own. Carefully observe participants as they perform their exercises. Children appreciate attentive adult supervision, as it encourages them to try each exercise, and ensures they are performing the movements properly. Knowing the instructor is watching serves as a major motivating factor for most young exercisers.

Example: "I will watch you as you perform the dumbbell curl exercise to the best of your ability."

4. Appropriate Assistance

Many boys and girls have difficulty mastering new strength-training exercises and require some help from the instructor. To assure proper exercise performance, give those participants a little manual assistance, actually guiding them through the desired lifting and lowering movements. Appropriate assistance can make the difference between successful and unsuccessful exercise experiences.

Example: "Let me guide you through your next three repetitions in the dumbbell curl so you can feel the correct movement pattern."

5. One Task at a Time

Give children only one task at a time. While providing a series of performance tasks may work with adults, this is typically confusing to children. Projecting one task at a time increases the probability that they will progress successfully through the exercise session. Although seemingly a simple thing to do, most instructors need considerable practice limiting themselves to one task at a time.

Example: "On this set of curls, I want you to breathe out as you lift the dumbbells from your thighs to your chest."

After this task is mastered, the next directive would be to breathe in as the dumbbells are lowered, even though this should occur naturally.

6. Gradual Progression

As indicated in the previous example, gradual progression should always be programmed, never assumed. Small steps in the learning process are essential for young people with little exercise experience. With few exceptions, do not introduce a follow-up task until the first task has been mastered. It is much more efficient to progress slowly and steadily than to progress too quickly and make mistakes that must be unlearned and rectified at a later time.

Example: "Now that you are breathing out as you lift the dumbbells, your next task is to breathe in as you lower the dumbbells."

7. Positive Reinforcement

Even the most outwardly confident children may experience some degree of uncertainty about their exercise efforts. Everything from their training weight loads to their exercise techniques to their muscle responses may convince them that they are not measuring up to expectations. But positive reinforcement can usually increase their self-confidence and satisfaction with the training program. This can come in the form of encouraging comments, personal compliments, or pats on the shoulder. Positive reinforcement is also an excellent means for maintaining appropriate social behavior in the exercise environment. Telling children they are doing a good job is one of the best ways to keep them doing a good job.

Example: "You are doing really well, Jim."

8. Specific Feedback

Positive reinforcement is much more meaningful when it is coupled with specific feedback. Try to provide relevant information to support your encouraging comment. Giving a reason for your positive reinforcement increases its value as an educational and motivational tool. Although it may not be natural for you to give positive reinforcement and specific feedback, these are important instructional techniques that are well worth developing.

Example: "You are doing really well, Jim, especially with your perfect breathing pattern, exhaling as you lift the dumbbells and inhaling as you lower the dumbbells."

9. Careful Questioning

For a variety of reasons, many children are reluctant to give information that could be useful in their program design. To obtain important feedback from young exercisers, ask them relevant questions. Try to ask questions that require a thoughtful response, rather than an unqualified yes, no, or grunt. Consider the critical difference between these two question-answer interactions.

Example One: "Jim, do you feel the effort in your dumbbell curls?" "Yes." "Good."

Example Two: "Jim, where do you feel the effort in your dumbbell curls?" "Right here in my elbows." "That's not where you should feel stress, Jim. Hold the dumbbells like this and see if you feel the effort in your biceps muscles instead of in your elbow joints."

10. Pre- and Post-exercise Dialogue

Do your best to sandwich each exercise session between an arriving and departing dialogue with the young participants. Spending a few minutes before and after each workout in enthusiastic conversation with the class members is time well spent, with many personal benefits. Greet each child by name upon arrival and welcome him or her to the workout. Do not let any participant leave class without saying goodbye and thanking him or her for taking part in the exercise program. These are simple but meaningful ways to make every boy and girl feel like a valued member of the training team.

Example: "Laura, thanks for coming to the fitness class today and congratulations on your excellent exercise form."

Attitude and Atmosphere

The primary purpose of a youth fitness program is to develop positive attitudes toward exercise. The fitness level children achieve is actually less important than their enthusiasm level toward purposeful physical activity. Due to the profound modeling effect that adults have on preadolescent boys and girls, the training atmosphere is a critical motivating factor.

In a large survey involving hundreds of adult exercisers, the three characteristics they value most in fitness instructors are: (1) knowledge of physical fitness and exercise science, (2) teaching ability, and (3) enthusiasm (Westcott, 1991). These same instructor attributes are important to young people, but most likely in the reverse order.

Children respond best to adult models they perceive as similar to themselves, competent in what they are teaching, and reinforcing in their behavior. The best way to be considered similar by your participants is to have a common interest, and perhaps the most appropriate common interest is their personal fitness progress. Remember also that children want to have fun, so you should ensure that every class is a fun experience. A great way to do this is to have fun yourself. This enhances your teaching satisfaction and provides common ground with the boys and girls in the program.

Competency is a major motivational factor for children, especially your ability to perform the activities and to demonstrate the exercises. Young people are much more impressed by what you do rather than what you tell them to do. Because modeling is the best means for influencing children's attitudes and actions, you should be well-prepared in every area and aspect of your instruction.

Reinforcement is the all-too-often-neglected component of an otherwise excellent exercise environment. To help children execute exercises perfectly, include corrective information as well as information that reinforces those things they have already mastered. For a better balance that strengthens the instructor-participant relationship, give at least one positive reinforcement for every corrective comment.

For example: "Jill, that was a very good set of dumbbell squats. On your next set, just try to hold your head a little higher and you will do even better."

Chapter Five

Programming Ideas

The key to successful youth fitness programming is to create safe, effective, and fun activities that inspire children and teenagers to develop lifelong, healthy habits. Youth fitness programs should not be a modified version of an adult fitness class, but rather designed to meet the needs and abilities of younger populations. Instead of focusing on the consequences of physical activity, understand the factors that motivate young people to be active. It may be helpful to survey adult members to find out what kind of activities their kids enjoy, or to have a brainstorming meeting with staff members who are tuned in to activities that kids like. In general, it is unlikely that "selling" the health benefits of exercise to children and teenagers will encourage participation. After all, how many times have your heard a 10-year-old say, "Thanks for the workout coach. My blood pressure is now under control."

While activity programs for children and teenagers should address the basic components of health and fitness, a variety of creative games and fitness activities will enhance athleticism, sports participation, and self-confidence. Do not forget the importance of play, which is one of the ways in which we all learn. Most youngsters participate in physical activity programs to make friends, learn new skills, and have fun (Borra et al., 1995, American Alliance for Health, 1999, 1 & 2).

The following suggestions will help you develop successful youth fitness programs.

1. You need to have experience working with younger populations. A common mistake is to assume that because you are wonderful with adults, you will be just as effective with children and teenagers. Some instructors lack the patience and understanding to work with children and teenagers. As a youth fitness instructor, you need to relate to kids in a positive manner and understand how kids think. You need to respect youngster's feelings and appreciate that their thinking is different from that of adults. You should also be a good role model and enjoy working with kids. Physical education or exercise science interns and trained volunteers that are innovative, enthusiastic, patient, and caring can help with instruction and program development. Staff training sessions can help you learn to work effectively with children and teenagers.

2. Show you care. Listen patiently, provide encouragement, address individual concerns, and help kids develop a positive sense of self. Think of your youth activity center as a community in which the instructors and kids form partnerships and feel connected to each other. Show you care about the kids and help them understand what is expected. Give kids a chance to succeed in at least one thing every day, and praise them when they do something right. Let kids know you missed them when they were absent, and if they do something wrong, help them understand that you still like them as a person. A child who feels connected to the program, makes new friends, and follows the rules cannot be the same child who disrupts the class or engages in negative behavior.

3. Follow established youth activity guidelines. Some parents and youngsters engage in ineffective and potentially injurious training methods. You must make every effort to dispel the myths of exercise gimmicks and provide sensible information that is based on scientific research. Further, games and fitness activities should be consistent with the needs and abilities of the participants.

4. Designate a safe exercise area exclusively for kids. The space should be clean, well-lit, and adequately ventilated. Depending upon the number of participants and size of the program, the designated space will vary. In some centers, it may be appropriate to use an aerobics studio or a squash court during after-school hours. Other centers may decide to build a training area exclusively for children and teenagers. Consider using the special features of your center, such as the pool or tennis courts. Or allot a section of your parking lot

during off peak hours for kids to have a safe place for in-line skating or scooter riding. To make it aesthetically pleasing, the indoor area should be brightly decorated with attendance charts and posters that relay positive and motivating messages. All equipment, such as step platforms, rubber tubing, and dumbbells, should be handled appropriately and stored safely when not in use. If weight machines or aerobic equipment are used, they should be easily accessible and evenly spaced to avoid injury.

5. Develop age-specific goals and objectives. Enhancing aerobic fitness or lowering blood pressure may be motivating factors for adults, but most youngsters just want to have fun, play with friends, and improve physical skills. In fact, since children are concrete thinkers, they see little value in prolonged periods of moderate to vigorous exercise. Improving a youngster's aerobic fitness or body composition should be the byproduct of games and fitness activities, rather than the primary goal. Instead of matching the child to the activity, match the activity to the child.

6. Start with a winning attitude. Choose an original name for your program that projects a positive image that is appealing and complimentary to kids. Structure noncompetitive games and activities in which everyone can participate and feel successful. Develop an encouraging atmosphere where kids are not fearful of trying new activities. For example, group activities are enjoyable and encourage participants to work together. When designing youth programs, frequently change the activities to keep the interest high. Of course, you are ultimately responsible for modifying games and activities to

match the various fitness levels of all the participants. With competent instruction and quality practice time, kids can learn the basic skills they need for successful and enjoyable participation in a variety of physical activities.

7. Advertise your program through various marketing avenues. Community-based youth fitness programs receive much attention when publicized through in-house newsletters, bulletin boards, brochures, and local newspaper articles. Photos of boys and girls in action can attract a lot of attention, and can help to stimulate interest in your program. Offer workshops and seminars to local schools, and provide an opportunity for school-age participants to see your facility. Invite parents and kids to a free information meeting, and give potential members an overview of your program and an opportunity to see your youth fitness center. Offer affordable youth programs and encourage parents to use the adult fitness center while their kids are working out. This not only encourages family involvement, but can increase your fitness center membership. Since parents often look for classes that coincide with the school year, schedule youth programs so they run during school terms. Keep in mind that school events, exam weeks, and vacation periods may affect attendance.

8. Meet and greet all participants in your program, taking the time to learn the names of all the kids. Remember, you only have a few minutes to create the idea that this is going to be a fun class with enthusiastic leadership. During the first week of class, start off with a name game and introduce the instructors and the participants to one another. Encourage the development of supportive friendships, as they can help to

provide motivation to continue participation. If children and teenagers feel that the instructors truly care about them, they are more likely to behave during class and follow instructions. At the end of every class, thank the kids for coming and offer a friendly goodbye.

Action Plan

Although kids can perform an endless number of games and activities, the following format works best for youth fitness programs offered on nonconsecutive days. Each class includes a 15-minute warm-up period, about 20 to 30 minutes of muscle conditioning activities, and 15 minutes of games and cool-down stretches. Since kids should not strength train two days in a row, alternative games and activities that focus on aerobic fitness, balance, coordination, and agility can be performed in place of the 20- to 30-minute muscle-conditioning segment if classes meet on two consecutive days. Following is a suggested program format for a two- or three-day-per-week class:

Active Warm-up

Begin each class with an active warm-up period that focuses on the large muscle groups. Aerobic dance, circuit training, obstacle courses, and simple games are not only popular, but are an effective means to prepare children and teenagers for muscle-conditioning activities. Ask a youngster to co-teach a warm-up session, then rotate the leaders so all kids get a chance. This helps participants feel empowered, which is linked to motivation. Also, ask the kids for their ideas so that they can help to design the warm-up activities. During the warm-up period, review the day's lesson plan and discuss class objectives. End the warm-up period with stretching activities.

Muscle Conditioning

This highly supervised phase of the program includes training exercises that are specifically designed to enhance musculoskeletal fitness. Following a review of proper training procedures, demonstrate the correct technique for each exercise. In addition to body-weight exercises, different types of training equipment such as child-size weight machines, dumbbells, medicine balls, and rubber tubing can be used. Teach children and teenagers how to perform each exercise correctly and to record their progress on workout logs. While some boys and girls may be tempted to see how much weight they can lift, remind all participants that the focus of the program is on learning new skills and having fun, as opposed to maximal lifting. No matter how big or strong a kid is, remember that boys and girls are still growing and that they may be experiencing new types of exercise for the very first time.

Participants perform about eight to 12 different exercises each session and record their repetitions and training weights on their own workout log to help down-play competition between participants. After all, peer comparisons inevitably do the most motivational damage to the kids who need the most encouragement. With the current focus on teaching youngsters lifetime fitness activities, the potential benefits associated with regular participation in supervised muscle-conditioning activities should not be overlooked.

Games and Cool-down Activities

At the end of every class, play a variety of games and activities that require only moderate amounts of skill and keep everyone in class moving. Games using balls, beanbags, and parachutes are inclusive and lots of fun. Kids look forward to this portion of the class and are encouraged to share their ideas with the instructors. While youngsters should not be allowed to play whatever they want, explain what type of games and activities are appropriate, and then allow them to choose an activity within that range. As the games or activities come to an end, quiet things down with stretching and relaxation exercises. Sometimes, you can celebrate a youngster's birthday in place of a game and play with the party balloons. At the end of every class, thank the kids for coming and provide positive comments about their performance.

Nutrition Break

What about addressing the poor nutrition habits of our youth? Consider including information about proper nutrition in a "Munch and Crunch" segment of the cool-down games and activities. "Show and tell" youngsters how to eat right through creative games and activities. Many kids are on their own to fix breakfast and lunch and often choose high-fat or high-sugar snacks. As part of your "Munch and Crunch" program, teach youngsters how to choose nutritious foods to enhance health and maximize performance. Allow parents to be part of the nutrition education component so they too can learn how to make healthy snacks and meals at home. If appropriate, provide a sample of healthy snacks such as bagels, low-fat granola bars, oranges, and flavored yogurts. Throughout the activity period, reinforce the importance of drinking water regularly during class, even if they are not thirsty.

A majority of kids do not want to spend time cutting up fruit for a salad or baking low-fat cookies. Your job is to develop strategies that motivate youngsters to develop healthier eating habits. The following ideas may help.

- Start when children are young and encourage them to try new foods. Children will often try a new food if they see an adult eating something that looks good. If a high-fat food is not offered, the child is more likely to opt for available healthy alternatives. Encourage parents to stock-up on healthy grab-and-go foods such as plums and raisins.
- Instead of "boring" classroom lectures, create games and fun activities that encourage healthy eating. Invite parents to be part of the nutrition education program, so they will plan healthy meals and snacks at home.
- Show kids how to jazz up leftovers.
- Provide children and teenagers with healthy alternatives to snacks like French fries and candy bars. Baby carrots with low-fat dressing, celery sticks with peanut butter, and apple slices with cinnamon are also easy to prepare, and kids love them.
- Be a good role model. If a youngster sees an adult eating high-fat snacks, children will mostly likely follow suit. Set a good example by choosing healthy snacks before and after class.

Chapter Six

Games and Activities

You have a unique opportunity and responsibility to positively influence the health and well-being of children and teenagers. Through age-appropriate games and activities, boys and girls of all ages and abilities can have fun, learn new skills, and be physically active for most of the class period. Realizing that high-intensity exercise does not need to be maintained for prolonged periods of time, use new and innovative strategies to promote youth fitness. Instead of focusing on increasing selected "outcome" measures of physical fitness, shift your attention toward encouraging a more active lifestyle.

When developing games and activities for boys and girls, keep in mind that participation in after-school physical activity programs is a personal choice. If participants do not understand the games or are unable to perform the activities, it is unlikely they will develop positive attitudes toward lifetime activity. And once a youngster develops a negative attitude toward physical activity it is difficult to change. Help youngsters understand the benefits of physical activity by choosing games and activities in which they can experience success and feel good about their accomplishments. Cooperative games and activities that are easy to perform and do not require a great deal of effort are particularly effective for children and teenagers who are overweight, sedentary, or have physical or mental disabilities.

Instead of forcing fitness on kids, teach them how to be physically active. Be enthusiastic about your job and take pride in what you do. Along with the primary objective of engaging youth in fun physical activities, you are also responsible for class management, quality instruction, transition periods, and skill development. Needless to say, the development of successful youth fitness programs requires preparation and coordination.

Recommendations for Success

Safety First

Before you begin teaching a kids' activity class, spend a few minutes thinking about safety issues, space requirements, and game formations. Remove potential hazards from the activity area and have a first-aid kit nearby. When necessary, modify a game or activity to create a safer alternative.

K.I.S.S.: Keep Instructions Short and Simple

Even the best games will not work if kids do not understand the rules. Avoid using vague terms, and realize that your pronunciation and choice of words can influence a child's ability to understand what is said. Take time to prepare your instructions ahead of time and pause strategically as you speak. Using explanatory devices such as physical models and "show and tell" demonstrations can assist in explaining a game or activity. You can role-play to show kids step-by-step what they should do. Do not teach complex games with multiple rules. If the element of fun is missing, reevaluate the intellectual requirements of the game or activity.

Alternate Low-, Moderate-, and High-intensity Activities

Explain to children and teenagers that exercise does not have to be continuous to be beneficial. Intermittent bouts of low-, moderate-, and high-intensity activity offer numerous health and fitness benefits. It also mimics the natural activity pattern of youngsters, which is typically characterized by haphazard increases and decreases in physical effort. Interval training (i.e., alternating high-, moderate-, and low-intensity games and activities) is a useful option for children and teenagers. For example, after a vigorous game of tag, choose a low-to-moderate intensity activity that will allow for adequate rest and recovery.

Spice it Up

Everyone can get bored if they perform the same activity day after day. Further, chronic, repetitive stress can result in an overuse injury. Use a variety of age-appropriate games and activities when working with children and teenagers. Not only will they enjoy the program more, but variety is a key to long-term exercise adherence.

Roles and Responsibilities

You are responsible for planning and developing safe physical activity programs that are age-appropriate. Create an atmosphere in which kids experience success and are not fearful of trying new activities. You are responsible for enforcing game rules and proper behavior (e.g., following instructions and telling the truth). Encourage kids to interact with each other in a positive manner. While recovery periods are needed throughout the class, try to shorten the transition time between games and activities to maintain interest and reduce the likelihood for undesirable behaviors.

Have Fun

Introduce activities that get kids excited. While "fun" is a difficult term to define, research suggests that factors such as participation, mastery, friendships, and positive relationships with the instructor all contribute to enjoyment (American Alliance for Health, 1999, 1 & 2). Games and activities should challenge, but not threaten, participants. If necessary, use smaller teams to provide participants with maximum play time. Awards can be used to support and encourage physical activity. When kids have fun and experience success, they are more likely to continue participating. Fitness activities or exercises should never be used as punishment.

Parent Support

When working with youngsters, get parents involved. Inform parents about the benefits of physical activity for kids, and let them know they should support their child's participation in a physical activity program. Send out a newsletter to inform parents about health fairs, safe exercise guidelines, summer activity suggestions, healthy eating habits, and other programs offered at your center. Allow parents to observe their kids participating in the activity program and, if possible, provide them with an opportunity to be physically active while their kids are in class.

Cooperation

Cooperative games and activities help kids develop good feelings about themselves and others in class. Unlike highly competitive games that are often characterized by aggression and a drive to win, cooperative games and activities help kids develop qualities such as compassion and sharing. While being on a sports team can certainly be a positive experience, problems arise when the focus shifts from learning new skills to winning. You may be surprised to know that most children prefer cooperative games to competitive games. And even if cooperative games do not have a huge impact on the competitive thinking of teenagers, they can at least show kids that physical activity does not always involve winning and losing. For example, instead of a traditional soccer game, try playing with two balls and take your eye off the scoreboard. Or simply chose a cooperative activity in which all partic- ipants can work together. Do not allow kids to pick teams because being chosen late in the selection process can have a negative effect on motivation and self-esteem. Last, consider the name of the game or activity when working with kids. Names such as "Steal the Bacon" are associated with negative behaviors in our society and should be modified.

Summary Checklist for Games and Activities

- Is the environment safe and free of hazards?
- Does the activity provide for differences in the skill levels of your participants?
- Are teams formed randomly or cooperatively, rather than by selecting captains?
- Can all kids experience success, and at the same time be challenged?
- Does the activity provide for maximum participation?
- Are kids encouraged to ask questions and communicate their concerns?

Use different types of equipment and a variety of training methods to keep activities fun and exciting. While you are only limited by your own creativity and enthusiasm, several low-, moderate-, and high-intensity games and activities can be easily modified to meet the needs and abilities of children and teenagers in your program. Some of these activities have been used by physical education teachers and youth fitness leaders for many years, whereas others have been created to match the abilities of kids. The references and Web sites listed at the end of this text will provide you with additional resources.

Warm-up Activities

The first 10 to 15 minutes of every class should prepare the participants for upcoming activities. A proper warm-up helps to prevent injuries by increasing body temperature and by stretching muscles and connective tissue (tendons and ligaments). A complete warm-up should include low- to moderate-intensity aerobic activities and stretching.

For example, 10 minutes of aerobic dance to music followed by several upper- and lower-body flexibility exercises is fun and effective. Depending on the needs and abilities of the kids in your program, try to incorporate hops, skips, and jumps into the aerobic warm-up period (Figure 25). In addition, once the children and teenagers have mastered basic aerobic movements, use a step platform (4 inches for children and 6 inches for teenagers) to increase the intensity of the warm-up. Also, ask the kids to hold and move a lightweight medicine ball (1 to 2 pounds) during the aerobic session to keep the warm-up fun and challenging.

Figure 25
Incorporating hops, skips, and jumps into the warm-up is a fun programming option and adds variety to your classes.

For variety, create a warm-up obstacle course using cones, hula hoops, balls, mats, agility ladders, and whatever else is available. The obstacle course should be designed for the skill level of the participants and modified regularly as performance improves. Kids can run around scattered cones, climb though hula hoops, bear crawl under supported ropes, side step through agility ladders, and jump along a "hop-scotch" game before skipping back to the start.

Games and Activities

Medicine Ball Workout

Lightweight medicine balls (about 2 to 4 pounds) can be used for muscle-conditioning activities. It is desirable to have balls of different weights and sizes to accommodate the abilities of all participants. Exercises such as an overhead press, front shoulder raise, front squat, and supine chest press can all be performed with medicine balls. In addition, medicine balls can make traditional abdominal exercises more fun. For example, once a participant has mastered the technique of the curl-up exercise, he or she can hold a medicine ball against the chests and toss the ball to a partner while lifting the head and shoulders off the mat. The partner then tosses it back as he or she returns to the starting position.

Cat and Mouse

This game is fun for kids of all ages and helps develop "core" strength in the abdominals and lower back. All players should stand in a circle with their feet about shoulder-width apart. One player in the group starts with the "mouse" ball and another player at the opposite side of the circle starts with the "cat" ball. When you say "go," the players turn their torsos from side to side to get the ball, and then pass it to the next player in the circle (Figure 26). The goal is to move the balls around the circle as fast as they can so the "cat" ball does not catch the "mouse" ball. Remind players that the ball must be passed (not thrown) and that the idea is to twist their upper body from side to side when moving the balls. Depending upon the age of the players, foam balls or light medicine balls (about 2 pounds) can be used for this game. For variety, reverse directions and add another ball to the game (the "dog" ball).

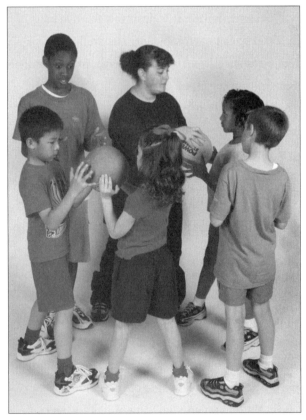

Figure 26
Cat and Mouse develops back and abdominal strength in kids of all ages and abilities.

Air Balloon

Balloons are inexpensive and invoke a natural desire to play. Kids can move the balloon around their bodies, though their legs and even pair up with a partner to perform a variety of side-to-side and over-and-under passing games. To play air balloon, participants should form a circle and hold hands. You toss the balloon into the circle and the players try to keep the ball in the air by using their head, feet, knees, body, and shoulders (Figure 27). Although they can use any body part to keep the ball in the air, they must hold hands throughout the game. Counting the number of times the balloon is kicked or tapped into the air adds to the excitement and fun.

Figure 27
Air Balloon is an inexpensive and fun programming option.

Beach Ball High

This game is appropriate for all ages and promotes balance, coordination, agility, and teamwork. Kids should scatter around a playing area that is free of potential hazards. One player tosses a beach ball in the air and then the group tries to keep the ball in the air for as long as possible (Figure 28). Remind the kids to hit the beach ball up in the air (and not directly toward each other) and encourage them to shout out the number of times the ball was hit. If the ball hits the ground the game starts over. As the kids improve, add more balls to make it more fun.

Figure 28
Beach Ball High encourages teamwork rather than competition.

Happy Hatter

This is a quieter game that enhances mental awareness and is fun for younger children. Players sit is a circle and one child who wears a hat is the 'Happy Hatter." This child points to one player in the circle and says "I'm the Happy Hatter and you don't have your hat on!" The chosen person must "freeze," showing no movement. If the chosen person can remain motionless for about 10 seconds, this player becomes the "Happy Hatter." To make this game more challenging, older players in the circle can stand on one leg and move their arms before they are picked by the "Happy Hatter." Try to give all players a chance to be the "Happy Hatter."

Snake in the Grass

Divide players into small groups, and ask one player to hold one end of a standard jump rope When you say "go," the player with the rope runs around the playing area moving and shaking the rope. The other players in the group try to pick up the end of the rope. The player who picks up the rope then gets to run with the rope. Give each player in the group a chance to run with the rope.

Parachute

Arrange players evenly around a parachute and ask them to firmly grasp the edges with both hands. Begin by having the players lift and lower the parachute using their upper body. Throw a few foam balls into the center of the parachute and encourage the players to "make popcorn" by using the parachute to lift the balls as high as possible. To change the intensity of the game, ask the players to lift the parachute with only one hand while the other hand is on the shoulder. Lots of different games and activities can be played by children and teenagers with a large, colorful parachute. For example, to play Chute the Ball, have the players stand around a parachute with one team on each side of the parachute. Place a large inner tube and two different-colored balls in the center of the parachute. When you say "go," the teams try to shake the parachute to get their ball through the inner tube to get one point. For variety, use more than two balls inside the parachute.

Capture the Chicken

This is a popular game that develops speed and quickness. If children and teenagers are paired with a partner of equal skill and ability, this game can be played by kids of all ages and abilities. Divide the players into two groups and have each group stand (or sit) in line at opposite ends of a large playing area. Assign each player a number and have them face the player in the other group who has the same number. Try to ensure that kids of equal ability are given the same number. Place a rubber chicken (or bean bag) in the middle of the playing area. When you call out a number, the two kids with that number run to the center of the playing area and try to bring the rubber chicken back to their team without getting tagged by the other player. Try calling two numbers at the same time and encourage players to pass the rubber chicken to a teammate without being tagged. A player can only be tagged if they have the rubber chicken in their hands, so they can pick it up and drop it when they need to do so. However, they cannot throw the rubber chicken over their team's line. Once a player is tagged or crosses their team's line, put the rubber chicken back in the middle of the playing area and continue. For safety, remind kids that they are not permitted to dive toward the rubber chicken as they run to the center. Also, remind them that there is a difference between a tag and a push.

Line Soccer

Kids of all ages and abilities can play this game, which develops speed, quickness, and kicking skills. The set-up for this game is similar to Capture the Chicken. The only difference is that instead of trying to bring a rubber chicken back to their team, a beach ball or foam ball is placed in the center of the playing area. When a number is called, one player from each team runs to the ball and tries to score a goal by kicking the ball past the opposing team, which tries to block the shot with their hands. After a player attempts to score, the ball is returned to the center and the game continues. For variety, try calling two numbers and encourage the teammates to pass the ball to each other.

Circle Soccer

Older children and teenagers enjoy this game, which develops agility, balance, and lower-body strength and endurance. Players should stand in a large circle with their feet about shoulder-width apart. The feet of players standing next to each other should touch (side to side). Ask the players to squat down until their thighs are about parallel to the floor (do not squat below parallel), and to hold this position and place their arms in front of their body. You roll a foam ball into the circle and the players try to score a goal by using their hands to hit the ball between the right and left leg of an opposing player. If the ball travels between players, it is considered out of bounds and the ball should be returned to the circle. Players can use their hands to stop a goal, but must try to maintain a proper squat position (e.g., head up and back flat) during the game. Take breaks as necessary, and always use a foam ball for safety.

Bola

Bola is a game that develops power, agility, and coordination, and is appropriate for older children and teenagers. The bola is made by tying one end of a long clothesline (about 8 feet) to a sock filled with sand that acts as a weight when the bola is swung. The group forms a circle and one player (or an instructor) stands in the middle of the circle holding the bola. The player in the middle turns in a circle swinging the bola while gradually letting out the rope so that it is long enough for the participants to jump over it. The bola should remain close to the floor, and as the players become more skilled, the speed of the bola can increase for a very fast-paced game. When a player misses a jump, a new kid swings the bola.

Hands Hockey

This game develops upper-body strength and endurance and is fun for older children and teenagers. Two players get in a push-up position (legs straight and arms extended) and face each other head to head (about 2 to 3 feet apart). A beanbag is used as a puck and each player's arms are used as the goals. One player begins the game by supporting his/her body weight with one hand and using the other hand to push the beanbag through the hands of the opponent. The beanbag must travel on the floor and the opponent tries to stop, catch, or deflect the bean bag. Each player gets a chance to score goals. Encourage players to alternate hands used to support their body weight. To make this game easier, the players can support their body weight on their hands and knees. To make it more difficult, the players can move further apart.

Runaway Train

This game emphasizes endurance, agility, balance, coordination, and teamwork. It is an action-packed game that young children enjoy. Groups of four or five children form a train by wrapping their arms around the waist of the person immediately in front of them. The front of each train attempts to link up to the back end (caboose) of any other train while trying to avoid being linked onto from behind by another train. If one train does hitch up with another, the two parts continue as one unit, trying to join up with other smaller pieces. Before long, all the small trains will be linked into one large one. The front engine can then try to catch and link up to the last car. Runaway Train is a good way to end up in a circle formation for a quieter game.

Fitness Relays

Different types of fitness relays can be created to enhance the speed, agility, balance, coordination and aerobic endurance of children and teenagers. Younger children enjoy a ball relay game in which they stand in a line facing the same direction and pass a foam ball over their heads, then between their legs, until the ball reaches the end of the line. The last player in line runs to the front of the line and continues the game. For older children and teenagers, different fitness relays using cones, scooters, balls, and agility ladders can be developed for added challenge and fun. Also, players can move in different positions during the relay race. For example, the crab crawl (lie on your back with weight supported by hands and feet), the seal crawl (lie on your stomach with hands directly below shoulders) and the turtle walk (lie face down with arms straight and knees off floor) can be used as part of a relay to enhance muscle strength and endurance.

Crows and Cranes

This is a high-energy game that requires a lot of running. Players should be divided into two equal teams and stand facing each other in two lines about 6 feet apart in the center of a large playing area. One team is the crows and the other is the cranes. When you shout "CROWS," all the crows chase the cranes, who turn around and try to run as fast as they can across a designated "safety line" about 20 to 30 feet away. When you shout "CRANES," all the cranes chase the crows. If a player is tagged before crossing the "safety line," he or she joins the other team (i.e., a crane who is tagged becomes a crow for the next round of this game). During the game, call out other animals like "crocodiles" and "cobras" to encourage the kids to listen carefully.

Circuit Training

Circuit training involves the performance of a series of six to 12 exercises with minimal rest between exercise stations. Depending upon the age and fitness level of participants, the rest period between stations can vary from less than 30 seconds to more than a minute. A variety of exercises that enhance aerobic fitness, muscle strength, flexibility, and balance can be included in the circuit. For example, an eight-station circuit can include the following exercises: push-ups, curl-ups, wall-sits, body weight lunges, jumping rope, hop scotch, one-leg stork stand, and a stretching exercise.

Tag Games

These running games are popular among children and teenagers and develop speed, endurance, and agility. Based on abilities and preference, different types of tag can be played.

Also, the size of the playing area can be modified for the age and abilities of the players.

Blob Tag: Two players hold hands and become the "blob," which runs around trying to tag the other players. As players are tagged, they become part of the "blob" by holding hands. Instructors should emphasize communication and should encourage the "blob" to work as a team. Other players are not allowed to break the chain of the "blob." For variety, try playing the game with two "blobs."

Tail Tag: Each player gets a "tail" (a 12-inch piece of cloth or a sock) and puts it in the back of his or her shorts at the waist. Be sure players do not tie the tail to a belt loop or pocket. When you say "go," the players run around and try to get the "tails" from the other players. Even when players have lost their "tails," they can still try to get the "tails" from the other players. When all of the players have lost their "tails," start the game again.

Triangle Tag: Three players in each group hold hands in the shape of a triangle and one of these players is "it." A fourth player on the outside of the triangle is also "it." When you say "go," the "it" on the outside tries to tag the "it" on the inside. Players in the triangle must stay together as they are being chased. Rotate the "its" until all players have had a turn. To make this game more challenging, ask players in the triangle to hop on one foot or run on their toes.

Index

F

facilities, 59–60
feedback, specific, 54
first-aid certification, 14
fitness education, 19–20
fitness relays, 81
flexibility training, 44–45, 72
food guide pyramid, 21
frequency of exercise
    endurance training, 41
    strength training, 32
fruits, 22
full-range movements, 31
fun, 69

G

games and activities, 63–64,
    73–83
    air balloon, 74
    beach ball high, 76
    bola, 80
    capture the chicken, 78–79
    cat and mouse, 73–74
    circle soccer, 79–80
    circuit training, 82
    cooperative, 60, 67, 70
    crows and cranes, 82
    fitness relays, 81
    hands hockey, 80
    happy hatter, 77
    parachute, 77–78
    runaway train, 81
    snake in the grass, 77
    tag games, 82–83
game supplies, 18

H

hands hockey, 80
happy hatter, 77
health and activity

questionnaire, 12
health check, 13
Healthy People 2010, 4
heart-rate monitoring, 42–43
hopping, 45, 72
hurdler's stretch,
    contraindicated, 17
hydration, 22–23

I

inner thigh stretch, 47
instructional guidelines, 50–55
intensity of exercise
    alternating low, moderate,
        and high, 68
    endurance training, 42–43
interval training, 68

J

joint flexibility, 45

K

K.I.S.S.: Keep Instructions
    Short and Simple, 68

L

leadership, 18–19, 61
leg extension, changes
    in for young exercisers, 27
line soccer, 79
locomotion skills, 43, 45
low-back and hip stretch, 47

M

marketing, 61
medical screening, 13
medicine ball, 63, 72, 73

modeling, 51, 56
"Munch and Crunch" program,
    64–65
muscle conditioning.
    See strength training

N

name game, 61
National Association for Sport
    and Physical Education, 8
newsletters, 70.61
newspaper articles, 61
nutrition break, 64–65
nutrition education, 20–23

O

obesity, childhood, 3
objectives
    age-specific, 60
    clarity, 51
obstacle course, 73
overuse injuries, 12

P

parachute, 77–78
parent involvement, 9–10, 69–70
patience, 59
physical activity, age-related
    decline in, 4
Physical Activity and Health, 4
play, value of, 19, 58
positive reinforcement, 53
programming
    format, 62–65
    ideas, 57–62
progression, gradual, 52–53
progression, strength training, 31
pull-downs, 29
pull-ups, 28–29
push-ups, 28–29

Q

quadriceps stretch, 49
questioning, 54

R

range, strength training, 31
reinforcement, positive, 53, 56
relays, 81
repetitions,
    strength training, 30–31
resistance level, strength
    training, 30
role modeling, 65
role playing, 68
rubber tubing, 63
runaway train, 81
running, 41, 82

S

safety, 13–14, 57–60, 67
Safety Action Plan, 14
scheduling, 61
seal crawl, 81
seated hamstring stretch, 44
sets, strength training, 31–32
"show and tell," 51, 64, 68
sitting hamstring stretch, 46
skipping, 45, 72
snacks, healthy, 22
snake in the grass, 77
soccer, line and circle, 79–80
speed, strength training, 31
Sports Safety Training
    Course, 14
sports skills,
    overemphasizing, 11–12
spotters, 15
staff training exercises, 19, 58
standing calf stretch, 44, 46
static stretches, 44

step platform, 72
stop-and-go games, 42
strength training
  exercises and frequency, 32
  guidelines, 29–40
  misconceptions and
      facts, 24–29
  and muscle strength
      changes, 26–27
  program segment, 63
  progression, 31
  range, 31
  repetitions, 30–31
  resistance, 30
  retention of gains, 27–28
  sets, 31–32
  speed, 31
  vs. body weight exercise, 28–29
stretching exercises, 44–45
supervision, 52

T

tag games, 82–83
tail tag, 83
testosterone, 25
triangle tag, 83
triceps and lat stretch, 48
trunk curl, 38
trunk extension,
  alternate sides, 39
turtle walk, 81

U

United States Olympic
  Committee, 14

V

vegetables, 22

W

walking, 41
warm up, 45, 62, 71–73
water intake, 22–23
weight-training equipment,
  18, 63
windmill, contraindicated, 16
workout log, 63
w-position, contraindicated, 16

Y

yoga plow, contraindicated, 17
youth
  current fitness status, 2–5
  time spent using electronic
      media, 3
youth fitness instructors
  involvement, 43
  leadership, 18–19, 61
  need for experience with
      children, 58
  roles and responsibilities, 69
  tips for, 19
youth fitness programs
  action plan, 62–65
  benefits of, 5–6
  guidelines, 6–9, 50–55, 59
  leadership and
      instruction, 18–19
  parent and community
      involvement, 9–10,
      69–70
  program considerations,
      11–12, 15–18
  program format, 62–65
  programming ideas, 57–62
youth fitness seminars, 19

References and Suggested Reading

Alter, M. (1990). *Sport Stretch*. Champaign, Ill.: Human Kinetics.

American Academy of Pediatrics, Committee on Sports Medicine and Fitness. (2000). Intensive training and sports specialization in young athletes, *Pediatrics,* 106, 154–157.

American Alliance for Health, Physical Education, Recreation and Dance. (1999, 1). *Physical Best Activity Guide: Elementary Level.* Champaign, Ill.: Human Kinetics.

American Alliance for Health, Physical Education, Recreation and Dance. (1999, 2). *Physical Best Activity Guide: Secondary Level.* Champaign, Ill.: Human Kinetics.

American College of Sports Medicine. (1998). The recommended quantity and quality of exercise for developing and maintaining cardiorespiratory and musculoskeletal fitness and flexibility in healthy adults, *Medicine and Science in Sports and Exercise,* 30, 975–991.

American College of Sports Medicine. (2000). *ACSM's Guidelines for Exercise Testing and Prescription,* 6th ed. Philadelphia: Lippincott, Williams & Wilkins.

Berenson, G. (ed). (1986). *Causation of Cardiovascular Risk Factors in Children: Perspectives on Causation of Cardiovascular Risk in Early Life.* New York: Oxford University Press.

Borra, S. et al. (1995). Food, physical activity and fun. *Journal of the American Dietetic Association*, 95, 816–818.

Borg, G. (1982). Psychophysical bases of perceived exertion, *Medicine and Science in Sports and Exercise,* 14, 377–381.

Centers for Disease Control and Prevention. (1997). Guidelines for school and community programs to promote lifelong physical activity among young people, *Morbidity and Mortality Weekly Report,* 46(RR-6), 1–36.

Centers for Disease Control and Prevention, Division of Nutrition and Physical Activity. (1999). *Promoting Physical Activity: A Guide for Community Action.* Champaign, Ill.: Human Kinetics.

Centers for Disease Control and Prevention. (1999). *Promoting Physical Activity: A Guide for Community Action.* Champaign, Ill.: Human Kinetics.

Cheung, L. & Richmond, J. (eds). (1995). *Child Health, Nutrition and Physical Activity.* Champaign, Ill.: Human Kinetics.

Corbin, C. & Lindsey, R. (1997). *Fitness for Life*, 4th ed. Glenview, Ill.: Scott Foresman.

Corbin, C., Pangrazi, R., & Welk, G. (1994). Toward an understanding of appropriate physical activity levels of youth, *Physical Activity and Fitness Research Digest,* 1, 8, 1–8.

Dietz, W. (1990). Children and television, in Green, M. & Hagerty, R. (eds). *Ambulatory Pediatrics IV,* Philadelphia, WB Saunders, pp. 39–41.

Drinkwater, B. (1995). Weight bearing exercise and bone mass. *Physical Medicine and Rehabilitation Clinics of North America,* 6, 3, 567–578.

Faigenbaum, A.D. (2000). Strength training for children and adolescents. *Clinics in Sports Medicine,* 19, 593–619.

Faigenbaum, A.D. (2001). Strength training and children's health. *Journal of Physical Education, Recreation, and Dance,* 72, 24–30.

Faigenbaum, A.D. et al. (1996, 1). Youth resistance training: Position statement paper and literature review. *Strength and Conditioning,* 18, 62–75.

Faigenbaum, A.D. et al. (1996, 2). The effects of strength training and detraining on children, *Journal of Strength and Conditioning Research,* 10, 109–114.

Faigenbaum, A.D., et al. (1999). The effects of different resistance training protocols on muscular strength and endurance development in children, *Pediatrics,* 104, 5.

Faigenbaum, A.D. & Westcott, W.L. (2000). *Strength and Power Training for Young Athletes.* Champaign, Ill.: Human Kinetics.

Faigenbaum, A.D., Zaichowsky, L.D., Wescott, W.L., Micheli, L.J., & Fehlandt, A.F. (1993). The effects of a twice-a-week strength training program on children, *Pediatric Exercise Science,* 5, 4, 339–346.

Falk, B. & Tenenbaum, G. (1996). The effectiveness of resistance training in children. A meta-analysis, *Sports Medicine,* 22, 176–186.

Flegal, K. (1999). The obesity epidemic in children and adults: Current evidence and research issues, *Medicine and Science in Sports and Exercise,* 31, 11, S509–S514.

Freedman, D. et al. (1999). The relationship of overweight to cardiovascular risk factors among children and adolescents: the Bogalusa heart study, *Pediatrics,* 103, 1175–1182.

Hamill, B. (1994). Relative safety of weight lifting and weight training, *Journal of Strength and Conditioning Research,* 8, 53–57.

Heidt, R. et al. (2000). Avoidance of soccer injuries with preseason conditioning, *American Journal of Sports Medicine,* 28, 659–662.

Hewett, T. et al. (1996). Plyometric training in females athletes: Decreased impact forces and increased hamstring torques, *American Journal of Sports Medicine,* 24, 765–773.

Janz, K., Dawson, J., & Mahoney, L. (2000). Tracking physical fitness and physical activity from childhood to adolescence: The Muscatine Study, *Medicine and Science in Sports and Exercise*, 32,7, 1250–1257.

Kaiser Family Foundation. (1999) *Kids & Media @ the new millennium* [monograph]. Menlo Park, Cal.: Kaiser Family Foundation, November.

LaRosa Loud, R. (1999). Take some of the work out of kids' workout. *Perspective*, 25,34–37.

Luepker, R. et al. (1996). Outcomes of a field trial to improve children's dietary patterns and physical activity. *Journal of the American Medical Association*, 275, 10, 768–776.

Marshall, S. et al. (1998). Tracking of health-related fitness components in youth ages 9–12. *Medicine and Science in Sports and Exercise*, 30, 910–916.

McKenzie, T., Alcaraz, J., & Sallis, J. (1994). Assessing children's liking for activity units in an elementary school physical education curriculum. *Journal of Teaching in Physical Education*, 13, 206–215.

Micheli, L., Glassman, R., & Klein, M. (2000). The prevention of sports injuries in children. *Clinics in Sports Medicine*, 19, 821–834.

Morris, F. et al. (1997). Prospective ten month exercise intervention in premenarcheal girls: Positive effects on bone and lean mass. *Journal of Bone and Mineral Research*, 12, 1453–1462.

National Association for Sport and Physical Education. (2000). Poor showing of California students on fitness assessment brings call to action. *NASPE News*, p. 9.

National Center for Health Statistics. (2000). *Health, United States. With adolescent health chartbook*. Online at: http://www.cdc.gov/nchs/products/pubs/pudshus/tables/2000/updated/00hus69.pdf.

Nationwide Personal Transportation Survey. (1997). U.S. Department of Transportation, Federal Highway Administration, Research and Technical Support Center, Lantham, Maryland: Federal Highway Administration.

Outerbridge, A. & Micheli, L. (1995). Overuse injuries in the young athlete. *Clinics in Sports Medicine*,14, 503–516.

Pangrazi, R. & Corbin, C. (1994). *Teaching Strategies for Improving Youth Fitness*. Reston, VA: American Alliance for Health Physical Education, Recreation and Dance.

Pangrazi, R. & Dauer, V. (1995). *Dynamic Physical Education for Elementary School Children*, 13th ed, New York: Macmillan.

Pate, R. & Hohn, R. (1994). *Health and Fitness through Physical Education.* Champaign, Ill.: Human Kinetics.

Payne, G. & Morrow, J. (1993). Exercise and VO_2 max in children: A meta-analysis. *Research Quarterly for Exercise and Sport,* 64, 3, 305–313.

Pratt, M., Macera, C. & Blanto C. (1999). Levels of physical activity and inactivity in children and adults in the United States: Current evidence and research issues. *Medicine and Science in Sports and Exercise,* 31, 11, S526–S533.

Rosengard, P., Sallis, J. & McKenzie, T. (1997). Thirteen ways parents can encourage physical activity in children. *Strategies,* 11, 2, 25–26.

Rowland, T. (1990). *Exercise and Children's Health.* Champaign, Ill.: Human Kinetics.

Safrit, M. (1995). *Complete Guide to Youth Fitness Testing.* Champaign, Ill.: Human Kinetics.

Sallis, J., McKenzie, T. & Alcaraz, J. (1993). Habitual physical activity and health-related physical fitness in fourth-grade children. *American Journal of Diseases of Children,* 147, 890–896.

Sallis, J. & Owen, N. (1997). *Physical Activity and Behavioral Medicine.* Thousand Oaks, Cal.: Sage.

Sallis, J. & Patrick. K. (1994). Physical activity guidelines for adolescents, consensus statement. *Pediatric Exercise Science,* 6, 302–314.

Sallis, J., Prochaska, J., & Taylor, W. (2000). A review of correlates of physical activity of children and adolescents. *Medicine and Science in Sports and Exercise,* 32, 5, 963–975.

Sallis, J. et al. (1993). Project SPARK: Effects of physical education on adiposity in children. *Annals of the New York Academy of Sciences,* 699, 127–136.

Sallis, J. et al. (1997). The effects of a 2-year physical education program (SPARK) on physical activity and fitness in elementary school participants. *American Journal of Public Health,* 87, 8, 1328–1334.

Sallis, J. et al. (1999). Effects of health-related physical education on academic performance: Project SPARK. *Research Quarterly for Exercise and Sport,* 70, 2, 127–134.

Smith, A., Andrish, J., & Micheli, L. (1993). The prevention of sports injuries of children and adolescents. *Medicine and Science in Sports and Exercise,* Supplement to 25, 1–7.

Strasburger, V. (1992). Children, adolescents and television. *Pediatrics Review*, 13, 144–151.

Trudeau, F. et al. (1999). Daily primary school physical education: Effects on physical activity during adult life. *Medicine and Science in Sports and Exercise*, 31,1, 111–117.

U.S. Department of Agriculture and U.S. Department of Health and Human Services. (2000). *Nutrition and your health: Dietary guidelines for Americans* (5th ed). Washington, D.C.: U.S. Department of Agriculture and U.S. Department of Health and Human Services, Government Printing Office.

U.S. Department of Health and Human Services. (1996). *Physical Activity and Health: A Report from the Surgeon General.* Atlanta, GA: U.S. Department of Health and Human Services, Centers for Disease Control and Prevention, National Center for Chronic Disease Prevention and Health Promotion.

U.S. Department of Health and Human Services. (2000). *Healthy People 2010: Understanding and Improving Health.* Washington, D.C.: U.S. Department of Health and Human Services, Government Printing Office.

Virgilio, S. (1996). A home, school, and community model for promoting healthy lifestyles. *Teaching Elementary Physical Education*, 7, 1, 4–7.

Virgilio, S. (1997). *Fitness Education for Children: A Team Approach.* Champaign, Ill: Human Kinetics.

Westcott, W.L. (1980). Effects of teacher modeling on children's peer encouragement behavior. *Research Quarterly for Exercise and Sport,* 51, 3, 585–587.

Westcott, W.L. (1991). Role model instructors. *Fitness Management,* 7, 4, 48–50.

Westcott, W.L. (1999). From myths to muscle. *Perspective,* 25, 20–25.

Westcott, W.L. & Faigenbaum, A.D. (1998). Sensible strength training during youth. *IDEA Health and Fitness Source,* 16, 32–39.

Westcott, W.L., Tolken, J., & Wessner, B. (1995). School-based conditioning programs for physically unfit children. *Strength and Conditioning,* 17, 2, 5–9.

Witt, P. & Baker, D. (1997). Developing after-school programs for youth in high risk environments. *Journal of Physical Education, Recreation and Dance,* 68, 9, 18–20.

Youth Health & Fitness Web Sites

Centers for Disease Control	http://www.cdc.gov
PE Central	http://pe.central.vt.edu
AAHPERD	http://www.aahperd.org
PE Lesson Plans	http://members.tripod.com/~pazz/lesson.html
SPORTQuest	http://www.sportquest.com
Games Children Play	http://www.gameskidsplay.net
President's Challenge	http://www.indiana.edu/~preschal
President's Council on Physical Fitness & Sports	http://www.fitness.gov
Fitness link	http://fitnesslink.com
Dole 5 a day	http://www.dole5aday.com
PE Lessons	http://educ.ubc.ca/dept/cust/pe
Cooper Institute	http://www.cooperinst.org
Fun brain	http://www.funbrain.com
Sport for All	http://www.sportforall.net
Strongkid	http://www.strongkid.com

NOTES

NOTES

NOTES

NOTES

NOTES

NOTES

NOTES

ABOUT THE AUTHORS

Avery D. Faigenbaum, Ed.D., is an assistant professor of human performance and fitness at the University of Massachusetts in Boston. He is a leading researcher and practitioner in the area of youth fitness and lectures across the country to fitness and sports medicine organizations. Dr. Faigenbaum serves on the editorial boards of several fitness journals and is certified by the ACSM, NSCA, and United States Weightlifting Association.

Wayne L. Westcott, Ph.D., is the fitness research director at the South Shore YMCA in Quincy, Massachusetts. He is recognized as a leading authority on fitness and has served as a strength training consultant for numerous professional organizations, including the President's Council on Physical Fitness and Sports and the American Council on Exercise. Dr. Westcott has authored 13 books on strength training and published more than 400 articles in professional journals.

Supported by
The American Council on Exercise®
www.acefitness.org

Operation FitKids, a nonprofit organization, is dedicated to enriching the lives of America's youth with enhanced education for healthy lifestyles and increased opportunities for physical activity.

For more information about how you can get involved with Operation FitKids, visit us online at www.operationfitkids.org.